DON'T MARRY BEFORE YOU ARE 30

A Book on Finding Success, Happiness and Love

JOY CHEN

wisdom tree

First published 2015

ISBN 978-81-8328-394-6

Published by
Wisdom Tree
4779/23, Ansari Road
Darya Ganj, New Delhi-110 002
Ph.: 23247966/67/68
wisdomtreebooks@gmail.com

Printed in India

A love letter to all the world's women

Contents

Whether we're single, married or divorced,
as women we all are blossoming into our own beautiful
adult selves.

Introduction

Leftover women are modern urban women most of whom have high education, high income and high IQ. They are nice-looking, but they are relatively demanding in choosing spouses so that they haven't found ideal partners for marriage.

—China Ministry of Education, 2007

In life, there's a season for everything. I got the career of my dreams, I got the man of my dreams, I got the children of my dreams. I got married at the age of thirty-eight. I got it all *because* I married late.

My own dear parents were horrified over my being a leftover woman. They could not understand how I could have gotten two graduate degrees without getting the one degree they coveted next to my name: Mrs. No matter how much I accomplished, our conversations revolved around 'The Big Issue':

Ma: Hi, Joy! My friends in California mailed me some news clips about you.

Me: That's nice.

Ma: But your father and I were talking about the fact that you're not living with us anymore.

Me: I haven't lived with you for fifteen years.

Ma: And you're not living with a husband.

Me: Because I'm not married.

Ma: Can you explain to me again what you're doing out there in California?

Me: Mom! Did you read the news articles? I'm improving the lives of millions of people.

Ma: But don't you know that a woman's most important job is to be a good wife and mother?

No, Ma. That's the way it *used to be*.

That was then, this is now

For centuries, men and women had clearly defined roles. Men were the heads of household, women the caregivers. Children were raised for these roles: Boys were trained to be strong and self-reliant, girls to be caring and compliant. We women lived to please others. In return for our service, we received a lifetime guarantee of stability and security. Marital unhappiness, if it existed, was kept discreetly behind closed doors.

That was then, this is now. We are living through a moment of radical change. This change is driven by three new developments:

First, the rate of divorce is exploding. Once known for its stable marriages, Asian countries like China suffer from the 'China-style divorce'. Based on a Tsinghua University survey, in 2009, 1.2 million Chinese couples got married but the same year 2.0 million couples got divorced as well.[1] A 2011 report in the BBC stated there had been a 100 per cent increase in divorce rates in India in the last five years.

Second, thanks to globalisation and advance in technology, our world is changing rapidly. The landscape in which we will live out our careers is fundamentally different from that which faced our parents. We're transitioning from a top-down world to a flatter world in which everyone has the opportunity to be a player. And the rate of change continues to increase. If you were to plot it on a graph, the line showing the rate of change as you move to the right would curve upwards steeply, with an ever-increasing slope. How well you fare in the twenty-first century will be determined by how well you master this dizzying rate of change.

Third, we've changed. For our mothers, marriage was necessary for survival, socially, if not financially. Now that we can survive on our own, we yearn for all the things that all human beings yearn for once their survival needs are met—to be loved, to have dreams, to have meaning in our lives.

For our mothers and grandmothers, a man was husband material if he had a job, didn't drink too much and didn't beat you. That doesn't cut it for us. We don't want just any man; we want a good man. We don't want a marriage based on duty; we want love. In the words of the idealistic Charlotte in *Sex and the City*, we want to 'dream the impossible dream!'

And that's just in the marriage department. In our careers, we want to soar as well. We worked, *so hard*, for all that education, and now we want to put it to use and do something. We don't want to just survive in society; we want to lead society.

And so we find ourselves at this strange in-between moment in history. We're surrounded by people who tell us that what we're looking for is unrealistic. They tell us to hurry up, settle down and make a baby. And yet we can't. Now that we want more, we can't go back to wanting less. No longer can we live out our lives by simply going along with what's expected of us.

We have dreams. Those dreams create a chasm separating us from centuries of women who've gone before. That chasm is cultural, social, emotional, philosophical and spiritual. We're the first generation of women who want it all.

Some women do get it all

Years ago when I was in grad school, I had heard the then University of California, Los Angeles (UCLA) Law School dean, Sue Prager give a speech to a women's group.

> Dean Prager: I am blessed to know several outstanding women who have made it to the top of industry. These women are truly incredible.
>
> 'Hooray!' We applauded.
>
> Dean Prager: I also know many *average* men, at the top of industry.
>
> The crowd fell silent. 'Yeah,' we thought, 'We know many of those, too'.
>
> Dean Prager: Someday, we'll know we've made it when *average women* can make it to the top of industry.

Right then, I wanted to know: Given the challenges that all women face, why do some women make it? What should I be doing differently?

Since then, the lives of my schoolmates have splintered in different directions. I'm forty-two now. My closest friends and I are lucky to be among the achievers. We call these the 'fabulous forties'. Gone are the turbulence and anxiety of youth. We're happy and self-assured like never before. All this makes us sexy to the right men. I love this from the mystery writer, Carolyn Heilbrun, about her protagonist:

> She has become braver as she has aged, less interested in the opinions of those she does not cherish and has come to realise that she has little to lose, that age above all, both for those with children and those without them, is the time when there is very little 'they' can do for you, very little reason to fear or hide or not attempt brave and important things.[2]

How did we get lucky when so many of our peers faltered? Here's what I've concluded: Women who achieve today don't have much in common with one another. They're not more talented, beautiful or smarter than everyone else. They have diverse personalities. They've made different life choices and they work in disparate fields.

What sets them apart from the rest is not who they are, but how they've approached their lives. The women who win—in business and in the business of life—are those who work hard and work smart.

Now for the scary part. My friends and I only happened to make smart choices. We made the choices we made without understanding the ramifications of those choices.

Often, it didn't even feel as if we were making choices at all, but rather, simply responding to life as it happened. In the words of the French novelist Andre Gide, 'The most decisive actions of life are most often unconsidered actions.' While our lives have turned out well, they very easily could have gone differently.

Previous generations of women had their lives mapped out for them. Suddenly, our lives are not mapped out for us. The possibilities ahead seem endless, and that's exhilarating. But at the same time, they're deeply confusing. Now that we can do anything, what should we do?

We're faced with a huge array of choices. Who should we marry? When? What jobs should we take? How should we spend our time? What should we believe?

We have zero visibility into the future implications of any these choices, and yet we'll be haunted by their consequences for the rest of our lives.

And our lifetimes will be much longer than those of our grandmothers. In China, for thousands of years, well into the twentieth century, life spans were very short. In the 1930s, life expectancy was only thirty-five years. By 2000, life expectancy had increased to seventy-one years.[3] Similar is the case in India. Now, given advances in nutrition and medical technology, you and I can expect to live into our eighties and nineties. This increase in life expectancy is so large that, in the words of Carnegie Corporation's Aging Society Project, in the twentieth century we've become almost a different species.[4] In other words, we'll live for a whole second lifetime and more with the choices that we make in our youth. Many of us have no idea what we'll want in five years.

We are a generation of women who never before have existed in history. Because we're the first, there's no one to guide us. It falls upon each of us to create our own lives of meaning and achievement. We have no examples but the ones we set for ourselves.

We're women, which is to say, we're crazy busy. But I believe it's urgent for us all to stop a moment and reflect. Because whether and how each of us succeeds will be based on the actions we take in our lives right now.

This is a book of strategy. I do not have all the answers. I have not learned all of life's lessons. I still have a lot of living to do myself.

Working on this book made me realise that so much of our experience is rarely spoken and yet shared by us all, and for that reason it's not been an easy book to write. How does one write about thoughts which reside only in our subconscious?

You may or may not agree with everything I have to say. My goal is not to convince you of anything, but simply to start a conversation, 'Here's what I think. What do you think?'

This is a book about my own evolution from a shy and scared young girl in America into a global citizen and take-no-shit older woman. It's about how I was appointed deputy mayor of Los Angeles at the age of thirty-one, and my later work—headhunting for global companies. And this is a book about love, about how I found Dave and how you can use advanced headhunting techniques to bag the man of your dreams.

In these pages, I lay bare the things I know now that I wish I'd known when I was starting out. My triumphs, my regrets. The things I would do over again if only I could. Recollections that make me laugh, memories that make me cry.

This is a book for you, those of you who have been loyal readers of my Global Rencai blog (*www.globalrencai.com*) and others whom I'm meeting for the first time now. You may find some of the chapter titles more eye-catching than others, but I encourage you to read this book from beginning to end, as I wrote each chapter to build on the previous ones.

I hope that this book encourages you to go out and find the right answers for your life. Above all, I hope that this book encourages you to be brave, to dare to ignore the rules, to go out and grab hold of everything in this world that you know you deserve.

A little about me

I am a woman, a former girl, a wife and now a mother to two baby girls. I'm Chinese by history, American by nationality. My mother is from Ningbo. My father is from Nanchang. They each emigrated to Taiwan and then to the States for grad school. They met and married in Boston. I was born on the East Coast, near Washington, DC.

As I was growing up, we were a family of Chinese-Americans, heavy on 'Chinese', light on 'American'. My parents, always worried about my brother and me becoming polluted by the immoral aspects of American culture, sheltered us carefully. They didn't allow TV in the house, discouraged us from spending time with Americans and made sure we stayed home when we weren't in school.

We socialised exclusively within the Chinese immigrant community.

My parents didn't make much money, so they sacrificed and saved to buy us a house in a good school district. That meant that we were the poor kids at a school that was nearly all-white.

As a kid, I was painfully shy. My English was horrible, so at school I rarely opened my mouth. These were the 1970s, and at the time, the world saw China as monolithic, poor and backward. This image reflected onto me as well. I was the strange, silent Chinese girl with the cheap clothes and Coke-bottle glasses.

All my teachers were white. Since none spoke Chinese, they didn't know that I spoke Chinese. All they saw was a kid who could not speak English, which to them meant a kid who could not speak, period. I was shunted off to the 'special needs' classes with the Down Syndrome kids. Later, as my English improved, I was sent back to the mainstream classes. But the social part of life remained challenging.

The other kids shouted racist epithets, 'Chink, go home to China!' and 'Hey slant-eyes! Ching ching ling long!' Since we didn't watch TV or listen to pop music, I had little contact with the media that other kids were consuming. So even after I could understand English as it was spoken, I couldn't keep up socially. The hardest was when the other kids were joking around. On the rare occasions that I came up with the right thing to say, it was always sixty seconds too late.

All those years, more than anything, I ached to be white. It wasn't about the skin colour, of course. It was about what being white signified. I thought that, if only I were white, I could be pretty, and rich, or at least normal, and then maybe the other kids would like me.

My father is a kind-hearted man. Throughout my growing-up years, he devoted his spare time to helping Chinese immigrants settle in the US. Our weekends were spent helping his new friends hunt for apartments and learn to drive.

In his professional life, he worked as a research engineer throughout his thirty plus years governmental career. My father was the hardest working person in his department. Each morning he was early to the office; each evening and weekend, he brought his work home. Whenever he travelled on business he would stay not at the three-star hotels with all his colleagues, but rather at the one and two-star hotels nearby, just to save the government money. Despite his receipt of several 'outstanding performance awards', and despite the fact that his master's degree was from Massachusetts Institute of Technology (MIT), they assigned him for research and never gave him leadership roles.

One evening when I was twelve or thirteen years old, my father said, 'Tonight is the evening of our department's annual Christmas holiday party.' Surprised, I asked why he hadn't gone. His response: 'Because when I go to those things, I never know what to say to other people.'

It was as if I'd been struck by a bolt of lightning. I suddenly realised two things. One, my father never would be as successful in his career as he should be. And two, the reason was that, in fact, my father was just like me—he didn't know how to talk to white people. I resolved to learn more, to figure out how society really works and what I needed to do in order to survive better and get ahead.

This journey took me so deeply into American society that I even entered politics. Now, as a corporate headhunter, I watch China's top students join global companies and then languish at the entry levels. From bookworms to worker bees, they progress no further than the insect stage. Seeing them work so hard with so little recognition reminds me of my father and his career.

Take control of your life

Growing up, I experienced Chinese-ness as an absence of whiteness and the easy life that I thought that entailed. Since then, I've come to revel in Chinese language and culture. Nothing now gives me greater joy than seeing my older girl form perfect sentences in Chinese.

I see now how growing up a misfit conferred upon me some unique advantages. As an outsider, I was in a unique position to understand how society really ticks, because when you're excluded there's nothing to do but to listen and watch. Feeling stupid, poor and ugly left me feeling at rock bottom. There was nowhere to go but up. Perhaps, tomorrow would be better. Feeling all alone, I made books my friends. I became a reader, learning voraciously from the world's great writers about vistas far beyond my own.

America can be unkind to outsiders, but if I'd struggled less, I wouldn't have had the formative experiences that led me later to a big career and life of my own. Looking back, I guess you could say that growing up different was the luckiest thing that could ever have happened to me.

We can't choose the circumstances into which we are born, but I suspect that we each have more power over our lives than we imagine. We all can take inspiration from the story of Oprah, who rose from a life of poverty and abuse to take control of her own destiny. In her words, 'I don't know what the future holds, but I know who holds it.'

Right now, you have within yourself everything—*everything*—you need to achieve your dreams, capture great love and live a life of purpose. And yet, since the day you were born, society has been conjuring a massive conspiracy to squash your spirit and make you a passive player in your own life.

Power is never given, only taken. It's time to establish the new rules of the game.

The poet Mary Oliver asks, 'Tell me, what is it you plan to do with your one wild and precious life?' That's the question that I pose to you at the start of this book. What is it that you plan to do with your one wild and precious life?

Go, make your dreams come true. And then, through your shining example, show the world, show us all, show me, how to really live.

Chapter 1

Why Young Women Falter

A woman needs dreams to ignite her passion.

—Jiang Wenli

Indian and Chinese women are the best educated, hardest working and the most promising talent in the world today. *Businessweek* in 2011 reported that enrolment at business schools in the United States is increasing because of women students from India and China![1] About 30 per cent of the 100,000 Indian students in the US are women, as former US Ambassador to India Nancy Powell was quoted in the media. And yet, young Chinese and Indian women are experiencing a crisis of insecurity, at precisely the moment when they should be taking advantage of all that education and doing well.

Who is stealing the confidence of young women? It's a question the world needs to confront, because in a global economy built on human capital, when the most promising among us falter, we all lose.

Girls start out smart and strong

The blogger Han Han had it right in *My Sharpness and Absurdity* when he wrote:

> The unique situation in China is that, kids are taught not to fall in love or have relationships during high school or even during college. But the moment their sons and daughters graduate from college, their parents demand that they immediately marry a partner who's outstanding in every way, ideally one who's already a homeowner. What a fantasy!

Han Han's perceptive words apply to all Indian and Chinese students, but especially to girls. As a mother of girls myself, I'm part of a special worldwide sisterhood. We know our precious darlings will face sexism, so we want them to feel extra loved, extra supported. While they're in school, we put them on the high-speed train to success. We shout, 'You can do anything, and don't let anyone tell you otherwise!' And excel they do, outstripping the boys in school, all the while shouting 'Hooray! Girls are better!'

So far so good.

But then they graduate and settle into their first jobs. Suddenly, we slam on the brakes. 'Don't be too smart, girls! You don't want to scare the boys!'

No wonder young women are confused. They're dizzy from whiplash.

Having interviewed thousands of candidates for executive jobs, I find that although young women are the best prepared, they have the least confidence. This lack of confidence then manifests itself in a disturbing trend: Throughout their twenties and thirties, increasing numbers of Chinese and Indian women fall off the leadership track, never to recover.

Why is an entire generation of otherwise outstanding young Chinese and Indian women faltering at the very moment when they should be taking flight?

The answer lies in the science of how dreams are made.

We may like to believe that as we mature our identities stabilise and we become set for life. But scientists tell us that's not at all how it works. As humans, we're social creatures. We depend on others to recognise us and affirm that what we're doing is right and good. This drive for affirmation is extremely powerful.

We're surrounded by people with opinions about what we do, and they're constantly offering their approval or disapproval. People who pursue socially approved ways of life receive a lot of affirmation. Those who don't, receive little. As a result, we're much more likely to pursue those goals approved by others. Recognition from others motivates us, energises us, focuses us and helps us to define ourselves. What did Boss think of my project? Does this dress make my butt look fat?

It's a lifelong process. Our hopes and dreams never become fixed. Throughout our lives, we reformulate our dreams and reshape our lives using the feedback we receive from others. In fact, says Harvard psychiatrist Anna Fels in her book *Necessary Dreams: Ambition in Women's Changing Lives*, 'The speed with which ambitions are reworked to fit changing social norms and therefore maximise social affirmation is nothing short of remarkable.'

Neurologists show how this process works through the

chemistry of our brains. When we receive social affirmation, our brain releases the chemical serotonin, causing us to feel secure, courageous, calm, resilient and self-confident. As long as we continue to achieve social success, our serotonin levels continue to rise, causing our self-confidence to rise.

And so, in the economy of social recognition, the rich get richer while the poor get poorer. Get yourself in a situation where you start succeeding and being recognised for your success, and you'll be motivated to be more successful. You'll start on a cycle towards greater success.

We, in HR, understand the power of recognition, and we build elaborate systems around institutionalising it to align employee behaviour with company goals. Recognition, after all, is the currency at stake when we dole out bigger job titles, corner offices, special parking spots, 'high-potential young manager' programme slots and employee mentions in the company newsletter.

What happens if nobody notices us, or worse, if our lives are met with disapproval? We falter. Neurologists show us how low status leads to low serotonin levels.

The leftover-woman stigma

Understanding then how fluid our identities are, we can better understand how damaging is the leftover-woman stigma. When our parents and friends start to withhold praise for pursuing our careers and focus instead on us getting married, our dreams shrivel, replaced by new dreams of playing a supporting role to one special man.

Marriage brings us legitimacy in the eyes of society. When we marry, in society's view, we're suddenly transformed from immature single girls into mature wives.

Sometimes, the pressure is overt, allowing us to simply roll our eyes and push back, 'Ma, that's nice for Julie, but my name isn't Julie!' But more often, the stigma of being a single woman is so subtle that we don't even feel it pervading our minds and spirits.

Recently, I met a young Asian woman earning her PhD at UCLA. Her extended family had pitched in to amass funds for her education in the States. She had overcome greater obstacles than Americans in the same PhD programme. She was probably smarter and doing better work than most of them. Her English skills were excellent. The headhunter in me was excited; I foresaw a bright future ahead for her.

I asked about her plans after school. She was unsure. I asked whether she planned to remain in the States or return to her home in Asia. She hesitated. Finally, she responded that she didn't know because she didn't have a boyfriend yet. She was waiting to get married and then she'd see where her husband wanted to live. She figured she'd take an easy lab job in the area in order to be more available to raise kids. In her words, 'I can't wait to get married. Then I'll feel like I'm really living. Right now, I feel like only half a person.'

Because she was waiting for marriage, I noticed, she wasn't pushing herself to write the papers, develop the mentors and take all the other steps she needed to be taking now to set herself up for the high-flying global career that she'd worked for all the way up until now.

As a headhunter and as a woman, I remained troubled by this conversation. At this crucial moment in her life, she was slowing down her career years before she faced any actual marriage or parenthood pressures. By her actions, she was guaranteeing herself fewer and less exciting career options throughout her life. She was inhibiting her own dreams.

This UCLA student is not alone. Everywhere I go, I meet outstanding young Asian women who are slowing down their careers now for the prospect of motherhood years down the line.

Don't do this. Keep pushing ahead in your career and don't slow down until you absolutely have to for the sake of raising your kids. If and when you do have kids, you may find that you don't have to slow down at all because of all the available childcare options. Or, at that point you may choose to slow down, but by then you'd have developed your skills and reputation to a level where you'd have many more exciting options even on a slower track.

For this half-a-person feeling, so common among modern women, we can blame a world that demeans and trivialises every aspect of a single woman's life:

> Oh, are you single? You're too picky. Self-centred, immature, lonely, desperate and miserable. You may have a fancy job, but your fancy job won't love you back. Are you having sex? Slut! Not having sex? Drying up! Are you devoted to your career? Just compensating for not being married. Are you happy? You just think you are. Without a husband you could never know true happiness. You will die alone.

It doesn't matter if your life is filled with great accomplishment as well as friendships and passion.

Society wants to define you by who you belong to. If you do achieve, you will be targeted. Don't take it personally.

Barbara Walters is a trailblazer, one of the world's first serious female TV journalists. In 1976, she became the first TV journalist, man or woman, to command a million-dollar salary. She has interviewed Indian Prime Minister Indira Gandhi, Chinese Premier Jiang Zemin, Russian presidents Boris Yeltsin and Vladimir Putin and every American president since Richard Nixon.

In 2004, she was interviewed about her four-decade career by another icon of TV journalism, Ted Koppel. After reviewing her accomplishments, he introduced the question he cared about most:

> 'Imagine,' he said, 'someone is softly humming in the background, "Is that all there is?" Was it worth it?'
>
> She quickly responded. 'Oh yes. I never thought I'd have this kind of a life.'
>
> He reminded her that she'd been married twice and divorced twice. 'Was it the job?' he asked. 'If it had not been for the job, would you still be married to one of those two men?'
>
> She replied she wasn't sure. But she had her daughter, and 'she is absolutely wonderful.'
>
> Wrong answer. He tried again. 'Do you ever sometimes lie in bed at night and say, "You know, maybe if I'd given up the job and focused on the family, that would have been…that would have been worth it"?'
>
> No, she didn't.

Ted Koppel is a skilful and persistent interviewer. But he could not get Barbara Walters to tearfully concede that she should have devoted herself to a husband instead of chasing down interviews with the world's most powerful leaders.

It's inconceivable that a reporter would badger a major male figure with: 'Was it all really worth it? Wouldn't you have been better off just being somebody's husband?'

I came across this interview while researching for this book. Reading it, I cringed. For much of my adult life, I was single and also deflecting similar questions from reporters. I thought it was just me. If I'd known I was in such illustrious company as Barbara Walters, perhaps I'd have had the nerve to fight a better battle.

If you think that getting safely married will suddenly make you official and let you into the club of legitimate achievers, then unfortunately, ladies, I have bad news. Public scrutiny will turn to whether you're giving enough care to your man.

Another Barbara, Senator Barbara Mikulski from my small home state of Maryland, was first elected to the United States Senate in 1987, the year I graduated from high school. She's now the longest-serving female in that august body commonly known as 'the most exclusive men's club in the world'. Here's what she says, 'If you're a woman running for office and you're married, they'll say you're not taking care of your man. If you're divorced, they'll say you couldn't keep your man. If you're single, they'll say you never could get a man in the first place.'

Turn on the television any evening, and watch the leftover-woman stigma play out across reality dating show.

All those skimpy dresses and flashing lights may make you feel like you're watching something very modern, but in fact the message to women is loud and clear and reactionary. A thirty-one-year-old female dating contestant comes on stage and the TV hosts react in horror, 'Thirty-one years old and not yet married?!'

Our society has taken a set of relationships which should be treasured—marriages—and turned them into the only relationships which matter at all in a woman's life. As a result, married women are considered normal and single women, abnormal. This attitude demeans and trivialises the lives of all women.

Actresses are always complaining about this. While the movies always offer multiple storylines involving major male characters, major female roles are limited to those of sex objects or love interests. After actresses pass the age of forty, the roles dry up.

The marriage pressure is relentless, and not just from the media or our mothers. Anytime I was at a dinner party, conversation turned to what others assumed was my #1 issue. It didn't matter how much I achieved or what else I was doing. Eventually, it all came down to: 'You're attractive, how does a woman manage to get to your age without getting married? What happened?'

That's akin to hearing of someone who was married at the age of twenty-two, opening your eyes wide and exclaiming, 'Married so young? Don't worry, honey, your divorce will come soon enough!'

And yet, all I did, all those times, was to look down at my feet and apologise that no, I didn't know why I hadn't married yet. So obedient!

Now I wish I could hit the 'rewind' button on my life, march back into all those media interviews and all those dinner parties, and when asked, 'Why aren't you married yet,' look them in the eye, smile wide, and say, 'Because, frankly, right now, I'm having the time of my life.'

I'd always felt annoyed at the leftover-women label, but it wasn't until I started to research for this book that I realised how deep and pervasive is the prejudice that leads us to recognise men for their contributions to society and women for their contributions to the home.

The long-term impact of all these messages is that we continue to enforce outdated roles, even after women have become educated. Women, who achieve professionally, receive less positive feedback, and the feedback we do receive is often laced with negative innuendo about whether we're also beautiful or whether we're doing enough in our roles as wives and mothers.

Femininity is not just a personality trait. The exclusive focus on being pleasing to others causes a huge loss of control over our lives. We can't control our looks, particularly as we age, and we can't control the people with whom we have relationships. Husbands stray, children grow up and move away.

Now we can understand the impact on young women's confidence when, after having spent years in school building skills of their own, suddenly their identities are torn from their control. By tearing down their dreams, society removes crucial support from their lives.

Not surprisingly, there exists a direct correlation between one's feeling of autonomy and one's overall well-being. For all of us, men as well as women, being competent and having some control over our lives translates into energy, optimism and confidence. Lack of control translates into discouragement and helplessness. The belief that we don't have control over our lives is inevitably calming.

Young women who graduate from school and face an abrupt withdrawal of praise, encouragement and reassurance for achieving, thus, naturally face a loss of self. While society has since abandoned the cruelty of binding our feet to keep us in the house, we've yet to abandon the practice of binding our souls, lest we actually step outside of the house and do something.

How I escaped the pressure

People often ask me, 'Wow, deputy mayor of LA! How did you do it?' Women tend to attribute their successes to luck and failures to lack of ability, while men attribute their successes to ability and failures to bad luck. Well, I'm not that ladylike, so I won't tell you that my achievements were due solely to luck. That said, it would be dishonest to conclude that my successes were entirely of my own doing.

In urban economic theory, there's an interesting concept called 'path determination'. Basically, history contains certain remote events—accidents—which become pivot points, causing massive other changes. As a result, those accidents take on historical significance. A classic example is the invention of the gas-combustion engine, which led to the development of the personal automobile, which in turn resulted in many other effects, such as personal mobility, traffic congestion, mobile air pollution and suburban sprawl throughout the world.

As I look back on my journey, I see how certain events and people were path-determinant, exercising outsized influence on my path.

When I was in high school, my father gave me a used Canon A-1 camera, and I jumped at photography as a medium for self-expression. Those days, before digital, everything about photography was expensive, so I took on an after-school job as a shop-girl to cover the cost of my supplies. Typically, I worked in the afternoons after school. After filling up each roll of film, I rushed to my high school darkroom to develop my negatives and make my prints by hand.

Upon entering the darkroom, I'd wait by the door for my eyes to adjust to the semi-darkness, and then, as I immersed myself, time would fast-forward rapidly. I still recall the pungent odour of the 'fixer' chemicals I used to stabilise the silvery images onto the photographic paper. By the time I emerged with prints in hand, often the sky would have darkened, saving my eyes from having to readjust to light.

With photography, suddenly I'd found an outlet for all my pent-up anxiety, hurt, loneliness and frustration, and also my joy, wonder and curiosity about the world. Even as I lacked the words to express myself, I made pictures to tell a thousand words.

One day, the high school photography teacher noticed my pictures drying on the darkroom clothesline and submitted one in a national photography contest at the world's largest museum complex, the United States Smithsonian Institution. Mine won, and for months it hung in the Smithsonian's Corcoran Gallery alongside art made by the masters.

That was nearly three decades ago. In retrospect, the award seems like a simple thing. But for me then, it was huge. Having always felt like a nobody, suddenly, I was a somebody. Somebody the world would take seriously. An artist. That sudden surge of self-confidence remained with me for years, even after I went off to college and set aside that beloved A-1.

During college in the late 1980s, I met the first of several powerful women who would have an outsized influence in my life. Yue-Sai Kan now is a bestselling author, journalist and business and cultural leader. At that time, she was already China's most famous woman as the host of CCTV's *One World*. One summer while I was at Duke, Yue-Sai welcomed me into her world as an intern for six weeks.

Our short time together made a lasting impression on me. Before then, the only adults I knew personally were the scientists and engineers in suburban Maryland and a couple of academics at Duke. But here was a woman who so gracefully combined Chinese and American cultures to educate and delight millions.

Yue-Sai taught me that a strong woman must be self-reliant. One day, I asked her about her real estate holdings, and she replied, 'Joy, never just have a job. What if they fire you?'

She's as generous with the individuals in her life as she is with the world. That summer, I had no place to stay in expensive New York City, and she welcomed me to stay in her own home. Two decades later when we reconnected, she barely even remembered me, over the years having mentored so many young women.

I'd imagine that few of you have actually met Yue-Sai in person, so I'll fill you in on the fact that she possesses a wicked sense of humour, as known by her many friends among the world's entertainment and political elite. If you ever get an invitation to meet Yue-Sai, jump at it, as she's simply sparkling fun.

She's the world's only Chinese woman who for over three decades has shaped society on a global level. I was deeply blessed to meet her during my impressionable college years. By her shimmering example, she taught me to turn my gaze heavenwards and dream big.

Several years later, when I was twenty-one, another pivotal event occurred. I graduated from Duke knowing one thing: I loved my family, but I needed to get away from that insular Chinese American community in order to spread my wings. So with no money and no connections, I moved to sunny Los Angeles (LA), 3,000 miles away. It was as far as I could go—any further and I'd be in the Pacific Ocean.

What I didn't know then was that LA is the Mecca for the world's refugees, dreamers and misfits. And I was a refugee, a dreamer *and* a misfit. I don't think there's another major American city where someone like me could have arrived at the age of twenty-one and become deputy mayor ten years later.

LA is a place radically unbound by orthodoxy. Here, the prevailing ethos is 'I'm OK, you're OK.' People don't care where you're from; they care where you're going.

I'll give you an example. On the East Coast, you'll

sometimes see a business card with a name containing a roman numeral, like 'John Edward Hancock IV'. That's a signal that here is a man with a family name so prestigious that they bequeath it down the line, and then they announce it to every person they meet. An East Coaster will receive a business card with a name written this way and treat its owner with appropriate deference.

An Angeleno, on the other hand, will receive this kind of a business card and peer suspiciously at its owner, thinking, what are you? Weak? Can't make it on your own? You have to tell me who your *great-grandfather* is? It's no accident that LA is the world's creative capital.

I arrived in LA with a dream: To become a successful real estate developer. I wanted to build innovative, environmentally-friendly communities, where people could live, work and raise their kids.

In the early years, I worked hard to gain my footing, living in tiny apartments and eating a lot of ramen. It wasn't always easy. I was scared a lot, often worrying over and questioning the choices I'd made. I attended graduate school at UCLA for my MBA in real estate finance and my MA in urban planning. UCLA awarded me a series of scholarships, and by juggling those grants, student loans and my continued work in real estate, I kept myself afloat.

Real estate development can be lucrative and after a few years, I started making pretty good money. My bosses told me, 'Joy, to be a developer you need to learn to drink Scotch.' So I learned how to drink expensive Scotch whiskey (Lagavulin aged sixteen years, splash of water, no rocks).

I bought myself a downtown apartment overlooking LA's Disney Concert Hall and had it designed by Annie

Chu, cutting-edge architect to platinum-selling music artists and major movie stars. Also a Chinese-American, Annie was generous to help me, since the tiny size of the apartment was matched only by the tiny size of my budget. We finished all the surfaces of the apartment using the cheapest materials, but in sumptuous colours. That apartment was more than a home. It was a haven. Anytime I had a bad day, I could always retreat to the calm and tranquility of my very own refuge.

Some days I felt on top of the world. When I travelled on company business, striding purposefully through airports in my favourite 'boots-which-made-me-feel-powerful'. Or when I rocked a Prada suit in strappy high heels (the key to Prada being not how hot it looks on a hanger but how hot it makes you look).

Those years were equal parts exhilarating and terrifying. Some days, I felt free, unencumbered and very grown up. Other times, I felt like I was just faking it, confused and all alone in the big city. When I think back to that time, I want to wrap that young me in a big hug.

All those lucky encounters set me up to soar

I was lucky that in those years, I received many hugs from another very special older woman. Thirty years my senior, Maureen Kindel was and is an influential businesswoman in LA. She's one of the world's most artful, generous, lively and charming personalities. Divorced, a mother and a grandmother, she loved to entertain, but hated organising events. So I jumped in, helping her with the details while she played hostess par excellence. Our Saturday night dinner parties and poker nights were legendary among

California's business and political elite. Over time, I became known as 'Maureen's Chinese daughter'.

Maureen understands power and how to wield it. From her, I learned how to connect with people of diverse backgrounds. During her late sixties, Maureen became so passionate about education that she returned to school to study it professionally. At the age of seventy-two, Maureen completed her doctorate in education. She intends to spend her next two decades as a leader for education reform.

Maureen is surrounded by a network of older women, married, single and divorced, who, like her, are living life to the fullest. For two decades, those women have offered me crucial support, reassurance, help, concern and affirmation. They were so wise and worldly and had so much fun, it was hard not to let some of that joie de vivre rub off on me. I started hosting my own parties in my own beautiful apartment.

People often ask me how I overcame my shyness. It didn't happen overnight. Aside from developing my English, the #1 thing I did was to develop a deep and abiding curiosity in other people. Over the years, I lost my self-consciousness in learning about others.

During my twenties, that curiosity drew me to people from widely disparate social universes. I made friends with businesspeople, artists, gay people, married-with-children people and many not describable in easy phrases. I could fit seventy in my apartment, assuming we filled every inch including the balconies and assuming everyone stood up, tummies sucked in and talking very loudly into the ear of the person wedged up alongside.

I became known as a connector, learning what makes

people tick and connecting them with others they should know. The more I connected people, the better I got at connecting people. A recent *Los Angeles Times* profile of me carries as its simple headline, 'The Networker'.

In my mid-twenties, I was appointed by the then mayor of LA as one of seven volunteer housing authority commissioners responsible for overseeing the city's extensive affordable housing portfolio. It was rare for someone so young to be appointed for such a prestigious post, but I had an especially suitable background. As a developer, I was steeped in the business of real estate. But unusually for a businessperson, I also was an expert in local policy, having studied urban planning at UCLA with LA as my research laboratory.

As women, it's easy for us to lose sight of our own possibilities. But the moment you taste power, you're different. Being a commissioner was my first opportunity to shape LA on a broad scale. The post also was important in demonstrating to me and to others that I could effectively serve the public. It became a stepping stone to higher office.

I share the same historical and cultural legacy as Asian women everywhere. And yet, thanks to an unusual confluence of events—my parents immigrating to the United States, my own move to LA—I've faced little of the suffocating pressure that confronts most Asian women.

Moreover, through a string of lucky encounters with important others, I received the support I needed to take flight.

For two decades, that love and affirmation has provided the wind beneath my wings.

Chapter 2

Down with Society's Fantasy of Marriage

I believe that a better life means more equality, freedom and dignity for everyone.

—Guo Jianmei

I believe in love. I believe in marriage. I am happily married to the man of my dreams. I want you to find love. If you want marriage, I want you to be happily married to the man of your dreams. All this is why I want to take down society's fantasy of marriage.

Just as society demeans every aspect of a single woman's life, it romanticises every aspect of the marriage institution. We're taught to believe that marriage is above all else what we should wish for, yearn for and work for. No matter whether we're happily married or miserably married, whether we or our husbands are faithful or not.

Society's fantasy of marriage goes something like this:

Marriage is a magical and transformative experience, the one truly important relationship in life. It is the one source of security that you as a woman can always rely on. Before, you hoped you were each other's everything. Now, you really are each other's everything. Marriage will make you whole and complete. Marry and you will never be lonely again.

Life's most profound decision

When you don't have a boyfriend, they ask, 'Why don't you have a boyfriend?' When you have a boyfriend, they ask, 'When are you getting married?' When you do get married, it's, 'When are you having babies?'

So you get a date. If you like him even a little, you begin trying to make a relationship work. You start pestering him, 'Where do you see us going?' 'Do you want to have kids?' You may date him for months. You may live with him, you may even marry him, knowing full well that he's far from ideal.

Why do you want to get married? Because your friends are getting married? Because society has bamboozled you into thinking you should be married by now? Because you're tired of being the third wheel when you go out with your girlfriends and their husbands? These reasons have nothing to do with the man you marry, and they bode an unhappy future. Without room in your relationship for the essential you, you and he both will be lonely forever.

Society tells you that since nobody's perfect, you should lower your standards and settle for what you can get. They tell you to get married as insurance against never finding anyone better. But marriage must be more than just an insurance policy. If you agree to the notion that you should lower your standards, you contribute to the belief that real love does not exist. Nothing could be more depressing or more insidious in women's lives. Whom you marry is life's most profound decision.

When we settle, we become complicit in creating a society full of loveless marriages and extramarital affairs. We start to believe that despite all the hard work that we put into our marriages, this is the best we could get, even when our husbands sleep around with other women. Then as we lower our standards, we enforce this same lovelessness on our children.

Given the grip the marriage fantasy has on us, it's amazing how many people are not living the fantasy. In the United States, for instance, the percentage of married couples has for the first time in history dropped below half of all households as a result of late marriage and high divorce rates. In 1950, married couples constituted 78 per cent of households, but in 2010, married couples constituted only 48 per cent of households. In 1950, 9 per cent of households consisted of an adult living alone, but now a remarkable 28 per cent of households consist of an adult living alone.[1]

These trends are profoundly making over American society in ways that we don't yet understand. For the first time in American history, most women are living without a husband.[2]

The trends in China are heading away from marriage at an even faster rate. While single people are rushing to get married, married people are considering whether to get divorced. Based on a Tsinghua University survey in 2009,

1.2 million couples got married, but the same year 2.0 million couples also got divorced.[3]

Today, marriage provides only the illusion of security. For many, marriage has been a net loss.

I've seen friends marry for love, and I've seen friends marry the nearest person when their alarm clock goes off at the age by which they think they should be married. What does it mean for a marriage to be a success? Merely managing to stay legally married till death do you part? Or something else? It's a peculiar paradox. We idealise marriage, and yet we're so bad at it.

Consider the implications. Well over half of us will become single through divorce. Of those who remain married, 50 per cent will become single by being widowed. Chances are, then, we'll be single more than once in our lives. Most of us now will spend the majority of our adult lives single. I'll repeat this because it's so important. Most of us will spend the majority of our adult lives single.

Let's then see singlehood for what it is—a normal stage of life, or perhaps the normal stage of life. Marriage, not singlehood, has become the transitional stage.

Society's fantasy of marriage wreaks havoc on women's lives. It pressurises us all into ill-advised marriages and then sets us up for nasty divorces, leading us into lives of financial, emotional and spiritual insecurity.

A generation of young children is now growing up in broken households across the world. We women often suffer greatly during divorce, but at least we can take charge of our lives and move on. Our children, on the other hand, cannot. When divorce occurs, they are victims in the truest sense. Vulnerable and defenceless, they often suffer from an enormous sense of rejection and guilt that they may have caused the split.

The impact on children of divorce can last a lifetime. In America, divorce became widespread in the 1970s, so my generation is the first to have grown up as the children of divorce. I continue to see the impact on my friends of their parents' divorces. Many have grown up afraid to love and fearful of life's possibilities.

Children can suffer such impacts even when their parents don't divorce but stay together in troubled marriages. And children are wise to our marital mistakes. In one study, half of young adults today whose parents stayed together said they may have been better off if their parents had divorced.

We can't fix a problem we don't understand, so let's take a closer look at society's fantasy of marriage. Given the gulf between the fantasy and reality of marriage today, why does the fantasy still exist? Two reasons. One is simple cultural lag. We women now can support ourselves outside of marriage, but this is a relatively recent phenomenon. Social dogma has yet to catch up.

But I believe that cultural lag is not the main reason for why the fantasy endures. The main reason we still hold fast to society's fantasy of marriage is that we want it to be true.

The fact that modern women now face so many choices in life is exhilarating and confusing. In fact, a superabundance of options can actually lead to anxiety, as psychologist Barry Schwartz shows in his book, *The Paradox of Choice: Why More is Less*. He cites a Columbia University study where a researcher went to a gourmet food store and invited shoppers to try out six different kinds of jam. Of those who sampled the jams, 30 per cent bought some. The next weekend, she set out twenty-four different kinds. On that weekend, more people tried the jam, but only 3 per cent of the samplers bought any.

When we make choices for our lives the stakes are much higher than the choice of flavours of jams. Right now, we're being confronted in our lives with choices, the consequences of which we'll live with for a lifetime. Worse, we have to make these choices with zero visibility into their future implications.

In life, as with the jam-samplers at Columbia, fewer choices can feel safer. Sometimes it feels more comfortable to have fewer choices. Sometimes it's nice just to be held and comforted, preferably by an older man. I know. I've been there. Wanting to be part of a couple, being in love with love, wanting to belong to someone. We take comfort in the notion that there's a predictable path through adulthood and that marriage leads to 'happily ever after'.

Marriage is not a magical elixir

Before researching for this book, I'd always assumed that married people are happier. After all, the media is always hyping studies that point to a link between marriage and happiness. I took all those media reports at face value and had even quoted from them on my blog.

But after reviewing the marriage research of Harvard social psychologist Bella DePaulo, I had to correct the blog. In her book *Singled Out: How singles are stereotyped, stigmatized, and ignored, and still live happily ever after,* Dr DePaulo dissects in meticulous detail, in more than 300 pages, the body of research linking marriage and happiness.

One problem that all the relevant research shares is the one discussed on day one of business school statistics class: Confusing causality with causation. In other words, although most (though not all) studies show marriage and happiness to be slightly positively correlated, no study has looked at the actual impact of marriage on happiness levels. It could well be that slightly happier people were the ones who got married in the first place. Another problem is that all of the studies look only at 'currently married people,' who are probably married because they like being married. They ignore the many people who were so unhappy with their marriages that they've gotten divorced.

Given all the ways the studies skew towards linking marriage and happiness, it's surprising how small the demonstrated bump in happiness actually is. The most-cited study shows a happiness bump of only 1.1 on a scale of 0 to 10. That's hardly enough to justify society's fantasy of marriage as leading from ultimate unhappiness to ultimate fulfilment.

Dr DePaulo also examines the lives of people who divorce, and here she finds a sadder story. While getting married and staying married doesn't much influence a person's overall happiness, it turns out that getting married and then divorcing is not as benign. People who divorce become less happy than they were before they were married, and many do not live as long as those who stay single or those who stay married.

Dr DePaulo concludes that it's better to be in no relationship at all than to be in a bad relationship. She concludes that the aim of her research is not to encourage or discourage marriage, but rather 'to urge more honest interpretation and reporting of the science of marriage and singlehood'. She believes it 'ethically reckless' to lead people to believe that marriage is the magical elixir to health and happiness when the science does not support that fantasy.

I believe in marriage as a lifetime commitment. But that doesn't mean I want to humiliate the majority of people in society who are single. To divide up the world between normal married people and abnormal single people is to make a false dichotomy. It leaves too many people on the outside looking in.

Married people, too, suffer from the marriage fantasy. Too often, I've been shocked with the news of divorce among my friends. 'What?' I'd think, 'Not them! They were like the constants of the universe! What happened?' Later, I would learn that they'd been struggling for years and were just maintaining a brave face for their friends. So sad. If they hadn't felt the pressure to prop up the marriage fantasy, if they hadn't felt such shame about the problems in their marriages, perhaps they could have enjoyed more support from those who care about them.

Single women envy married women, but in my experience married women envy single women too. When I was deputy mayor, my stay-at-home-mom friends sometimes would visit me at City Hall. They'd see all the ways we were changing the world and envy me for my life filled with friends and meaning. By contrast, they were struggling to find their own direction.

Not leftover, just blossoming

The *Wall Street Journal* reports that the more women are paid, the less eager they are to marry. A study of 3,000 singles found that women earning high incomes are almost twice as likely to want to remain unwed as women earning low incomes. 'What is going to happen to marriage and childbearing in a society where women really have equality?' Princeton demographer Charles Westoff wonders. 'The more economically independent women are, the less attractive marriage becomes.'

For this reason, I love actress Li Bingbing's suggestion that we change the term 'leftover women' to 'flower blossom women'. This pun is especially apropos. Whether we're single, married or divorced, as women we all are on the journey towards blossoming into our own beautiful adult selves.

Indeed, a review of fourteen years of US National Survey data showed an 11 per cent jump in happiness among single women in their twenties and thirties, and a 6.3 per cent decline in happiness among married women of the same age. 'If marriage had ever served to boost personal female happiness', the researchers concluded, then 'those effects apparently have waned considerably in the last few years.' A *Women's Day* magazine survey of 60,000 women found that only half would marry their husbands again if they had to do it over. In 2006, the Gallup Organization found that 68 per cent of divorced or widowed Americans plan to remain unmarried.

Among groups whose opinions on marriage are especially instructive are those women experienced enough to be immune to society's fantasy of marriage and wise enough to make their own choices. Who are these mythical beings? Financially stable (the financially stable part is key) women in their thirties, forties, fifties, sixties and seventies who are divorced or widowed and can marry again if they choose.

I happen to know many such women who are single again after decades of good or bad marriages. After an initial period of adjustment, it's as if their newly-single status led to their rebirth. They're no longer susceptible to grand illusions about marriage. Their lives are exciting, stable and peaceful, and packed full with friends, hobbies and volunteering. After decades of putting others ahead of themselves, they're now loving their freedom. Many are actively dating.

In the words of Danish writer Isak Dinesen, 'Women, when they are old enough to have done with the business of being a woman, and can let loose their strength, must be the most powerful creatures in the whole world.' In general, their attitude towards love and re-marriage is, 'It would take a truly incredible man to make it worth giving up my current life!' Hear that? The voice of a happy and confident woman. It's the attitude to which all single women should aspire, before attempting marriage.

Neither singlehood nor marriage is an automatic ticket to bliss. And yet the marriage fantasy is deeply ingrained in our lives in a million subtle ways, in the conversations we have, in the media we're surrounded with. All those little messages add up, making society's fantasy of marriage feel like a universal truth, making it hard to examine.

No other human being can make you whole. To put that much pressure on anyone is simply unfair and will result in sadness and frustration for everyone. Whether or when a woman marries is a choice that should be hers alone. Why should society care so much anyway? Marriage as an institution should be strong enough to withstand any woman's decision to delay marriage without everyone else seeing it as a threat.

Don't live your life based on what other people claim is normal or acceptable. Don't make crucial life decisions based on outdated social dogma. Don't get caught in the trap of needing to be married or have kids by some age that someone else has set for you.

Men are taught to choose. Women are taught to be chosen. Being a professional headhunter gave me the step-by-step knowledge I needed to choose among men. But it was because I'd first built a life of my own that I had the confidence to choose.

Marriage is not a cure-all for the problems of your life. It's not a magical and transformative experience. It's not a refuge to escape to when you feel lost and incomplete. Anyone can get married at any time. Marriage is just another human relationship that one can enter or exit at will.

We all need security. But the only security that's lasting is the security you find within yourself. Autonomy is the basis for intimacy. Don't wait to find someone. You are someone. Marriage does not complete you. You complete you. Love is profound. Marriage is not.

Chapter 3

What is Love?

We focus too much on the outside world and too little on the inner heart.

—Yu Dan

I don't know what business school is like where you are, but where I went to school, 'real men' (like me) took real estate finance. Money was power, or so we thought, so those who managed the money had the power. My class of thirty-two contained one other woman. In our imagined hierarchy of the universe, finance-related majors reigned, while marketing and HR were 'for the girls,' which is to say, people lacking the IQ for math. We brandished our HP 12c financial calculators like little badges of honour.

It's taken me a lot of years, a lot of living and a lot of metabolising of that living to realise that my view of the world was upside down. The reality is: Math is for wimps. Math is the easy part. It's much harder to deal with people. 'Deal' as in interact, negotiate, lead, love or have any kind of real human interaction with. The winners in society are the people who know how to deal with people.

Queen Elizabeth and the power of empathy

Once upon a time, there was a princess named Elizabeth. She was in line to be queen of England. Princess Elizabeth had a problem. She had two outstanding suitors. It was time to choose.

> Of suitor #1, she said, 'Every time I'm with him, I feel *he*'s the most fantastic person in the world!'
>
> Of suitor #2, she said, 'Every time I'm with him, I feel *I'm* the most fantastic person in the world!'
>
> Which one did she choose?

That's right. Suitor #2 is now known to the world as her husband, Prince Philip, while suitor #1 has been lost to history forever. Queen Elizabeth and Prince Phillip now have been married for over six decades.

We can learn from them both. From Elizabeth, we learn how to be dignified. She did not try to earn the love of a man. She was the future queen! She did the choosing. Any man would have considered himself lucky to be chosen.

You may not be a queen, but here's the funny thing about life: If you think like a queen and act like a queen, people will treat you like a queen. We teach people how to treat us.

From Prince Phillip, we learn to seduce. Becoming the world's most fascinating, beautiful, accomplished person will get you only so far. The key to true success, in career as well as in life, is the ability to seduce.

There's a trend these days towards the notion of

'personal authenticity'. Everyone says 'Just be yourself'. They're wrong. It's not enough to just be yourself. To succeed in anything, you also need to think about how other people will interpret you. And isn't it always nicer to make people come to you?

Yes, as a matter of fact, it is. Do you know anyone like that? A woman who's like a male-magnet, exerting an irresistible pull on all the men? Or someone who's always at the centre of all the fun parties? Or someone who simply floats up into management, leaving everyone else stuck in the trenches? What they all have in common is a skill called 'empathy,' the capacity to recognise and share someone else's feelings. Empathy is the ability to:

- Understand the characters, perspectives, motivations and values of other people.
- Form deep and meaningful personal and professional relationships.
- Respond to others in appropriate and effective ways.

We all carry around agendas with the people in our lives. With the boss, it could be, 'Give me a promotion!' With a boyfriend, 'Take me on vacation!' But it's easy to focus so much on our agendas that we don't receive the emotional cues which can help us achieve our agendas.

School teaches us to master areas of knowledge. But when it comes to relationships, it's the energy between two people that makes all the difference. Empathy is the most important skill you need in career and life.

Here's what I see as one of the underlying problems today. We lack skills in empathy. This isn't due to our language or culture, but to how we've been raised.

Our parents, sincere in their rush to help us excel, exhorted us to work first and play later. We took away the message that how well we perform is more important than who we are. And so, many of us grew emotionally numb, strangers to our own selves. In the words of one blog reader:

> They refer to our generation as 'rubber people'. We have no pain, no happiness and no dreams, since most of us aren't living a life but a status (marriage status, employment status, income status, etc.). We've been compared with one another since childhood, by our exam score, the school we attended, the degree we hold and the salary we earn. We're anxious because all our value is reflected in those quantitative indicators. We care about how others think of us more than what value we create. Therefore our dreams, if we still have any, are likely to be based on external comparisons, like being super smart or owning a big company or having a lot of money, rather than devoting ourselves to something from within our hearts.

When approval is meted out for excellence, we start to believe that our worth as human beings is tied to external measures of performance. All of this results in an almost unbearable amount of pressure. The high divorce rate among the eighteen plus is a function of the fact that first we were divorced from ourselves.

By contrast, I often look at my American friends with wonder. So happy and carefree! How can they be so happy and carefree? Indeed, our lack of training in empathy emerges perhaps most sharply when we attempt to interact with Westerners. It was when I was a student, lost and alone at Duke, that the Japanese British writer Kazuo Ishiguro published his searing novel *The Remains of the Day*. I cried all the way through, identifying with the protagonist, Stevens, who aims to be the perfect British butler to a carefree American master.

Stevens is emotionally repressed, and his style is formal and courteous (that was me!). He overthinks the few interactions that he has with other people (me again!). His speech is limited to the necessary, practical requests made of him by his employer, and he gets horribly confused whenever attempting to discuss emotions or to joke ironically. In his imposed silence, he stands to the side as his employer hosts dinner parties. He says to himself:

> It is curious how people can build such warmth among themselves so swiftly. It is possible these particular persons are simply united by the anticipation of the evening ahead. But, then, I rather fancy it has more to do with this skill of bantering.

I was Stevens. I too recognised that 'in banter lies the key to human warmth', and yet in my interactions with Americans, bantering always was the hardest part.

Feel and think before you say or do

We all start somewhere and, perhaps, that somewhere is farther behind than people from other, more emotionally open societies. But empathy is a skill which we all can develop. Here's how:

- **Be genuinely interested in other people.** Management guru Peter Drucker was famous for his theories, so it's fascinating what he said about people, 'I was always more interested in people than in abstractions. People are to me not only more interesting and varied but more meaningful precisely because they develop, unfold, change and become.'

- **Stay humble.** Some people's humility decreases as their wealth and power increase. This is a dangerous tendency. Humility is necessary for empathy.
- **Broaden your areas of knowledge.** To be an agile thinker and capable conversationalist, become a student of the world.
- **Talk about what they want to talk about.** Focus 80 per cent of the conversation on the person you're speaking with. Find out about her interests, and talk about those. You'll find that everyone is interesting, everyone has a story—and everyone likes talking about themselves!
- **Always listen at the most involved level.** Researchers identify three types of listening:
    - Level 1: Listening deeply, actively observing, interpreting non-verbal cues and sensing the messages behind the words.
    - Level 2: Hearing all the words but disregarding non-verbal cues such as body language and tone.
    - Level 3: Listening to only parts of the conversation, tuning out or getting distracted for the rest.

Our lives are so busy that we all get stuck listening at level 2 or even level 3. We all can become better listeners by practising listening at level 1, for all the conversations in our lives.

The fact that I'm raising my girls with an emphasis on empathy is not because I'm smarter or better than other parents, or that I love my children more. Rather, it's because I've had a life filled with diverse influences—including having read up on child development—that Dave and I try to nurture in them all that makes them special: Their own feelings, ideas, talents and interests.

For little ones, big feelings can be scary. Our big baby is now in her 'terrible twos'. One moment she's playing happily with her sister, then suddenly her little face reddens, screwing up into a scowl. Her lower lip juts out, she inhales and she blows, a little volcano spewing a big mash-up of anger, frustration and fear. Rather than say, 'It's OK! Don't cry!' we try to help her identify her feelings. We ask, 'What is it? You seem mad. Are you mad? I think I know why. Is it because your younger sister grabbed the toy away?'

Helping her voice her feelings has the effect of turning on a giant release valve on the side of her volcano. Her little shoulders relax and she starts to calm down. In his intriguing book, *Brain Rules for Baby*, neurologist John Medina describes the physiological effects that such soothing strategies have on a baby's brain.

Babies are born ready for relationships, recognising and responding naturally to emotions. Parenting that helps a baby identify her emotions actually helps her neural architecture develop towards lifelong emotional stability. A baby parented this way will become an adult with better self-control, fewer incidences of depression and anxiety disorders, greater empathy, deeper and richer friendships and many more friends.

By contrast, some adults never grow up, remaining stuck emotionally in their 'terrible twos'. They go through life as if in a trance, closed, confused and easily overwhelmed. They're limited in their ability to function as managers, spouses, parents or even as friends. Their feelings, undifferentiated and unexpressed, become a fiery stew of anxiety.

Being able to identify and express feelings is a baseline tool for dealing with life. That's because our feelings dictate how we look at the world. Feelings matter. The more we recognise them, the more control we have over them. Here's the conflict: When we pretend feelings don't matter, they become repressed, and then they really matter. They become exaggerated, and that's when things really go wrong. We women tend to internalise our pain, but men externalise theirs, discharging their anxiety through sudden jolts of anger, sometimes with dangerous effects on those around them.

A top executive recently shared with me this management lesson, 'If it feels good, don't say it.' Do not ever react emotionally. Learn to shift from being emotionally reactive to emotionally responsive. When you're in a stressful or emotional situation, hit the 'pause' button. Before reacting, make the time to:

- Pay attention to yourself. Identify your feelings and verbalise them.
- Postpone your comments, actions or decisions until you've had a chance to sort things through.

Don't just feel about a situation, or just think about a situation, but take the time to do both.

Feel and think before you speak or do.

I can't tell you how useful that 'pause' button has been to me over the years. I think back to every time that I lost my temper, or said something or did something that I was embarrassed about later, and wish I'd paused first to process the situation. Many times, I've staved off a bad situation using these little words, 'I need a little time to think about this.' Most times, people are flattered that I take the conversation seriously enough to want that time. And I've always benefitted from the pause.

Shifting from reacting to responding takes time and practice. But becoming good at this has great benefits, both for us and for the people in our lives. Self-awareness is a deep sense of understanding of who we are, why we do what we do and a commitment to taking responsibility for the results of our actions. With self-awareness, we make better decisions, accomplish more and earn other people's respect.

To manage others, we must first manage ourselves. As we all push towards better integrating our thinking with our feelings, we'll all become better leaders, parents and lovers.

Sometimes I still get uncomfortable with all this mushy talk of feelings. And so I appreciate the work of psychologist John Gottman, who's developed a reassuringly mathematical framework for relationships. Dr Gottman has spent decades observing couples and measuring their facial grimaces and blood pressure changes when they interact. He's quantified all those interactions into an index for marital conversations (hooray, ratios!).

Different interactions carry disproportionate weight. For example, expressions of contempt register at minus four. Expressions of disgust receive minus three. Whining comes in at minus one. On the plus side, a display of affection—a smile of sympathy, a touch—registers at plus four. A marriage becomes risky for divorce when the ratio of positive to negative interactions falls below a ratio of 5:1.

Just by watching a videotape of a couple in the first few moments of a conversation about an area that they argue about, Dr Gottman can predict with 94 per cent accuracy whether that couple will later divorce. His term for the long-term happily married is 'the masters of marriage':

> When the masters of marriage are talking about something important, they may be arguing, but they are also laughing and teasing and there are signs of affection because they have made emotional connections. But a lot of people don't know how to connect or how to build a sense of humour, and this means that a lot of fighting that couples engage in is a failure to make emotional connections. We wouldn't have known this without the mathematical model.[1]

While Dr Gottman's mathematics focus on married couples, I think we can extrapolate his findings to all relationships. In any relationship, establish a 5:1 ratio of positive to negative interactions. For every criticism or negative comment, make sure you have at least five compliments and positive comments. What matters is the overall savings account of positive and negative interactions.

Each time you make a positive interaction, you're

making a deposit into the account which can be withdrawn on a rainy day. When you have large savings of positive feelings, you can use that to offset hurt feelings when someone is criticised. Make sure everything balances out in the end.

When in the drive to excel we all become disconnected from ourselves and others, the inevitable result is a society where everyone views everyone else as a competitor and an obstacle to our own success. The inevitable result of that is an India or China where today we feel like we can't trust anyone, and where we're all tired and trapped and scared of what might come next.

To me, that means that in India or China today, empathy matters even more. Empathy will lead to success in all aspects of our lives, because everyone is tired, everyone is scared.

Taking the initiative to truly connect with another human being is an incredibly powerful first step. At an even deeper level, empathy is the start of filling our lives with the love and trust and true human connection that's missing in our world today.

What is a soulmate?

Readers sometimes ask me what I think about soulmates. 'What is a soulmate? Do you get just one?'

I believe the world contains several people who can be your soulmate. You choose one. At first, you're two independent people. When you make the decision to commit to your future together you start to intertwine your lives. Over time, your bond becomes symbiotic, like yin and yang. You become soulmates over time.

Falling in love is easy. Staying in love is another matter. Those early tidal waves of emotion are not enough to sustain a lifetime. This can be really confusing because no other experience is quite as intoxicating as falling in love. And we can fall in love well before we're mature enough to evaluate someone as a potential soulmate. Teenagers fall in love with passion and abandon.

Some couples are so busy gazing into each other's eyes that they don't realise it's more important that as they look to the future, they're looking out in the same direction. Here's the typical recipe for modern marriage: Date someone you happen to know who happens to like you. After a period of time, marry him. Then make a lot of compromises and work really hard to try to make it work. When it doesn't work, divorce him.

We always hear about how marriage takes a lot to work, and you have to work hard to stay together. In fact, marriage is quite easy if you do two things: (1) Marry the right guy, and (2) Develop the skills for love.

I want Dave to know that he's the world's most fantastic person. My job is made easier by the fact that I believe that he is the world's most fantastic person. In my daily interactions with him, I try to put aside my personal tendencies towards impatience, narrow-mindedness and egotism, and instead to practice empathy.

Having started out as an argumentative, fact-driven person, I used to get carried away in arguments with Dave. I'd be convinced that I was right, and I wanted to prove it. After a while, though, I realised that, if my goal is love, the goal of winning an argument is pointless. Sometimes, he and I simply see things from different points of view, and that's OK.

What's made all this much easier for me is the realisation that, within our marriage, my goal is love. Love for myself, love for Dave, love for our daughters. And the most efficient way to reach that goal is to develop within myself the skill of empathy. In this way, I've found marriage to be a great training for life. The result is a better marriage and a better me.

Marriage is nothing like dating. It's actually more like a mundane small business in which you are co-partners and co-employees. That may sound boring, but actually it can be really nice, if you're hitched to the right partner.

For your little company to succeed, you must believe in each other and trust in each other's good judgment. You must agree on the direction of your company and the values by which it will run. You must decide how your company will make money, and how to spend it. You must identify what tasks must be done, and who will do what. Unlike in any other small business, however, you both must commit to being co-owners and co-employees in this company for the rest of your days on Earth.

When we first married, I thought that I could not love another person more than I loved Dave, but each year our love has continued to deepen. We've been graced with the arrival of two baby girls who make our hearts burst. But at the core of our family is still just the two of us. Every morning starts off right when I wake up to find beside me my best friend and lover.

My life is filled with many friends, but I'd rather

be with Dave than with anyone else. Lots already has happened in our marriage, but we have many memories yet to be made. When I'm with Dave, my heart sings. The world is a brighter and more joyful place. We share and plan our lives together. We laugh at the same things. The prospect of growing old with him makes me glad.

Great love affairs should not be defined simply by whether or not they exist within the legal institution of marriage. Love can come between a man and a woman, with or without sex, and within or outside of marriage. I'm frustrated by how American politics is so polarised around the issue of whether gay people should be allowed to marry. The way I look at it, it's a beautiful thing any time two people love each other regardless of their sexual orientation.

Was marriage the right choice for me? Yes. Does that mean it's the right choice for everyone? Not necessarily. All dogma aside, I have friends who are happily married, unhappily married, happily single and unhappily single.

The magical elixir of love

Important to my relationship with Dave is that he's my best friend but not my only friend.

As modern women today, we don't need marriage to survive, but we do need love in the form of true connections with others. I agree with actress Rene Liu when she says, 'I believe that the friendship between females is as indispensable as the relationship between male and female; neither the friendship nor the relationship is replaceable; I enjoy them both.'

The New York Times' bestselling author Tom Rath of the worldwide polling company The Gallup Organization once set out to study the roots of long-term homelessness in America. When he began his research, he assumed that most homeless men and women were homeless as a result of alcohol or drug addictions or mental illness. But when he and his colleagues interviewed homeless men and women in depth, they discovered that addictions and other problems were more a symptom than a root cause.

The men and women who remained homeless for decades had one thing in common: A lack of healthy friendships. More than anything else, they were 'friendshipless'. Being without a home was only the most obvious and visible part of their plight.

Rath and his colleagues then turned their attention to those who had emerged from homelessness, to see what enables some people to conquer homelessness. What they found was just as striking. Those who overcame their homelessness had found someone—a volunteer, a long-lost family member or someone else—who believed in them.

Rath condensed his homelessness research and his analysis of over eight million interviews from the Gallup Organization international databases into the book *Vital Friends: The People You Can't Afford to Live Without.*

Whom we surround ourselves with is very important, since we become like our best friends. He concludes that friendships are among the most fundamental of human needs, 'Without friends, it is very difficult for us to get by, let alone thrive.'

It's no wonder that prisoners held in long-term solitary confinement suffer mental-health damage. As humans, we're social creatures. Having a broad social network makes us happy and gives us a sense of community. Our brain controls many of the mechanisms responsible for disease, and just as stress can trigger ill health, friendship protects us.

Not only do we need friends, but it matters what roles our friends play in our lives. In order to feel satisfied and to reach our full potential, says Rath, each of us needs these eight specific types of friends:

> Builders motivate and coach us. Champions stand up for and praise us. Collaborators share our interests and passions. Companions are always there for us. Connectors introduce us to others. Energisers are our fun friends. Mind Openers share ideas with us. Navigators advise and help steer us.

No one person can play all these roles at once, and one mistake people often make in relationships is asking that of one person—often a boss or a spouse. Having a range of friends helps us to develop different parts of ourselves and to become more complex and autonomous as individuals. Bottom line: The wider and deeper your friendships, the better.

Given the cold and often brutal world we live in, it can be easy to forget the importance of love. That leaves a terrible void in our lives, because we really need love. We need love in a variety of human relationships. By deeply understanding others through empathy, we can learn to love them, and by loving others, we can become better, more complete versions of ourselves.

We'll all live longer, healthier, more productive and successful lives when we experience true friendships every day. That may sound simple, but at the end of the day, love is a matter of life and death.

Chapter 4

You Just Wanna Marry a Rich Guy, Right?

If a woman depends on a man, she will not have her own dreams. In today's society, men love women who own their own selves.

—Yang Lan

Don't tell me. You just wanna marry a rich guy, right? Don't tell me rich men need love too, so why should that not be you?

Don't tell me you love him, but between us girls, you wouldn't love him as much if he didn't have all that money. Right?

You don't have to tell me because I know. I've been there. Once upon a time, I just wanted to marry a rich guy.

By the time I graduated from Duke in 1991, China was opening up to the world, and with its economic prospects rose my social prospects. Asian women became trendy in America. Correspondingly, Americans' view of me evolved from strange and ugly to intriguing and beautiful. Naturally, I welcomed this happy turn of fortune.

And so I dated a succession of men, some rich and powerful, others less so. Because most were older, it was easy to try on each one's already structured life. This was literally manifested in how I dressed. Some guys liked rocker chicks while others preferred the classy conservative look. I was like a chameleon changing my skin colour to suit my surroundings. By the time I hit thirty, my eclectic wardrobe included many pieces which were simply not 'me' and which I'd never wear again.

When I think back to each of those relationships, my conclusion is, 'Am I glad I didn't marry him!' That's not to say that any of those men would not have made a fine husband for someone else, but rather that back then, I myself was not mature enough to commit for a lifetime.

No amount of searching would yield what I needed, because I was looking for things in men that I needed to give myself. We hurt both ourselves and others when we make ourselves over to suit someone else. As we become more independent, we naturally begin to look for more in our relationships.

Mr Right doesn't want to be your sugar daddy

A New York City woman once posted this personal ad:

> I'm a beautiful (spectacularly beautiful) twenty-five-year-old girl. I'm articulate and classy. I'm looking to get married to a guy who makes at least half a million a year. I know how that sounds, but keep in mind that

a million a year is middle class in New York City, so I don't think I'm overreaching at all.

I am looking for marriage only. Please hold your insults—I'm putting myself out there in an honest way. Most beautiful women are superficial; at least I'm being upfront about it. I wouldn't be searching for these kinds of guys if I wasn't able to match them—in looks, culture, sophistication and keeping a nice home and hearth.

A wealthy Wall Street guy responded:

Your offer, from the perspective of a guy like me, is plain and simple a crappy business deal. Here's why. Cutting through all the BS, what you suggest is a simple trade: You bring your looks to the party and I bring my money. Fine, simple. But here's the rub, your looks will fade and my money will likely continue into perpetuity. In fact, it is very likely that my income will increase but it is an absolute certainty that you won't be getting any more beautiful!

So in economic terms, you are a depreciating asset and I am an earning asset. Not only are you a depreciating asset, your depreciation accelerates! Let me explain, you're twenty-five now and will likely stay pretty hot for the next five years, but less so each year. Then the fade begins in earnest. By thirty-five, stick a fork in you!

So in Wall Street terms, we would call you a trading position, not a buy and hold, hence, the rub marriage. It doesn't make good business sense to 'buy you' (which is what you're asking for) so I'd rather lease. In case you think I'm being cruel, I would say the following. If my money were to go away, so would you, so when your beauty fades I need an out. It's as simple as that. So a deal that makes sense is dating, not marriage.

Separately, I was taught early in my career about efficient markets. So I wonder why a girl as 'articulate, classy and spectacularly beautiful' as you has been unable to find your sugar daddy. I find it hard to believe that if you are as gorgeous as you say you are that the $500K hasn't found you, if not only for a try-out.

By the way, you could always find a way to make your own money and then we wouldn't need to have this difficult conversation.

I hope this is helpful, and if you want to enter into some sort of lease, let me know.

At the end of the day, the perfect rebuke to a proposed bargain between a woman's looks and a man's money came from one particularly clear-eyed male.

I know. It can be fun to have a rich boyfriend. He takes you to the best restaurants, jets you around to glamorous cities and buys you fancy clothes.

But that rich guy, particularly that older rich guy, already has a life. When you insert yourself into his life, you lose your own life. Being his girlfriend, or even his wife, and raising any children that he might have becomes your life. If that's not bad enough, then don't be surprised if later you lose your new life too, when your beauty diminishes and he runs off to find a mistress.

Don't aspire to live out your entire life tethered to a man for economic life support. You will never be the equal of any man in a relationship if in your heart you are not confident that you can live well with or without a man. At age seventy-seven, the feminist leader Gloria Steinem speaks of the need for women to plan ahead:

> Everything I did seemed temporary, because when I was growing up, you were supposed to marry and therefore didn't plan ahead. We [think] that who we marry and our children are going to dictate our plans.... I finally am free of the fantasy of ending up as a bag lady because I did begin to save money after I turned fifty. So I do have the confidence now that I'm probably going to be able to support myself.

What's most touching about this quote is not that she won't end up a bag lady, but that the knowledge that she won't end up a bag lady is what gives her confidence for life.

I'm friends with many rich and powerful men, and this is what they have in common: A man with any self-esteem (the only ones you should consider) has no interest in being somebody's sugar daddy, and he's smart enough to recognise a gold-digger from a mile away. He'll not allow himself to be used without using you back. After all, says Mr Wall Street, why buy when you can lease? If you want someone who's outstanding, then be outstanding yourself. A good man wants a true partner.

I'm like you. I want to live in a comfortable home and I like nice things and I want my children to have everything. The way to gain money and power over our lives is by first earning it ourselves.

Make your own money, ladies. He needs to know that you're there because you want to be, and also that you can leave at any time you choose.

What if things don't work out? What if he disappears for whatever reason? You need to be able to keep going. IBM executive Ruoyi Zhou shared with me what she tells her daughters:

The most valuable advice Grandma impressed upon me is 'what's most important for a woman is to be independent.' What I would like to add for you girls is: Do not have children until you are absolutely certain you can support them financially, emotionally and physically all by yourself.

But what if I find a rich guy who *wants to* support me?

A blog reader once wrote to me, 'But what if I've found a rich guy who wants to support me? He wants me to get my MBA and then he'll support me to start my own business! Shouldn't I marry him?'

The Jewish Austrian theologian Martin Buber in his 1923 book, *I and Thou,* describes human relationships as taking two forms. The first is 'I-It', treating the other person as an object, seeing him only in terms of what he can do for you. The second is 'I-Thou', seeing him as a subject, and thus being aware of his needs and feelings as well as your own.

When you see a man as I-It, that's not loving him. That's just a circular way of loving yourself. Your attitude does not recognise his uniqueness, but only his usefulness to you. Substitute another guy who is equally compliant and you'd marry him.

Lots of people marry for money. Doing so may even make you feel sophisticated, très chic. But sometimes you can be too smart for your own good.

Don't avoid society's push to get you into a loveless marriage only to put yourself into a loveless marriage. When you objectify someone by marrying him for money you're not just objectifying him, you're objectifying yourself. That's because you're the catch. But there's no way to recognise the value of you if you're just looking to marry a rich guy.

Marriage narrows down all the possibilities of your life. Don't diminish the possibilities by binding yourself to a man you don't really love. You deserve more.

What if he has a business reverse? What if someday you have to support him? If someday you and he were poor, would you still love him just as much? With the economy spinning as rapidly as it is, big money comes and goes in the blink of an eye. A guy who's rich today can be poor tomorrow, and a guy who's poor today can be rich tomorrow. When I was in the real estate business I was surrounded by entrepreneurs who one day were worth tens of millions and the next day were broke.

When I say you should marry for love, that doesn't mean you have to be poor. The way to look at men and money is this: Marry someone who shares your values about money. If you want to build wealth, don't marry someone who does nothing but play video games and fritter away money. If you don't care about money and things and want to make just enough to support your passion to travel lightly and have interesting experiences, then marry someone with the same attitude.

Motherhood is a complicated bargain

Planning for life is hard for everyone, but it's especially hard for women today. It can seem unnatural and unromantic to consider the benefits and risks of forming a family before doing so. So people enter marriage with only the vaguest of good intentions. 'We both want to have fulfilling work. We both want kids. We will share in childcare responsibilities. We believe in equality.' Rarely do people enter marriage having had a realistic discussion of the logistics of launching a family.

But a marriage that works well for two people gets much more complicated when #3 or #4 comes along. They always tell you that parenting changes your life forever, and by the time I became a mother, I'd seen many friends become mothers. And yet, still I was stunned at the amount of time, love, wisdom—and money—that children soak up.

Parenthood has many joys but also many deprivations. From minute to minute, parenthood is intense, time-consuming and all-encompassing. Unlike any other job, however, it goes on for twenty-four hours a day, 365 days a year. When one is a new parent, it's hard to plan a day, much less a career. It's when we have kids that many of us as women realise we've made a complicated bargain.

As women, most of us don't want to bear the sole responsibility for doing the parenting. We want to enjoy our time with the kids, but we also need the other parts of our lives.

Compared with men of previous generations, today's husbands are doing much more of the housework and spending much more time with the kids. And yet, we still have a long way to go to achieve equality. Most women still do much more of the housework and child-rearing. For most of us, motherhood means we get two full-time jobs rather than one.

When men step in to help with any of the duties that society considers ours, they receive social approval. I always laugh when, on the weekends, my guy friends write online status updates like, 'Wife at the hair salon. I'm babysitting two children all by myself!' I want to comment, 'Hey buddy, when they're your own kids, it's not called babysitting. It's called parenting.'

Men are more likely than women to take breaks for personal activities, like exercise, eating and hobbies. When was the last time you heard of a mother with young kids going out to play a round of golf?

Sociologists find that men and women respond differently to the challenges of combining work and family. While multitasking—juggling kids at the playground with a client on the smartphone, for instance—men get a heady 'superdad' feeling, while women just feel stressed. These findings are from the two-year '500 Family Study' published December 2011 in the *American Sociological Review*, the journal of the American Sociological Association.[1]

Fathers, when watching their kids, are more likely to engage in 'interactive activities' that are 'more pleasurable than routine childcare tasks.' When mothers have childcare duties they're more likely to take the kids along on errands, drive them to activities or supervise their homework. When fathers get home from work they report reduced stress and improved moods as their stress lightens. But when mothers get home from work to start their 'second shift,' they report no such emotional boost.

Study leader Barbara Schneider says that this new data helps explain a paradox. While men's contribution to household work has increased, this has not resulted in happier mothers.

No wonder there are so many demoralised mothers who complain about all the stress in their lives. The life of a married woman with children is much harder than that of a married man, a single man or a single woman.

Women suffer the costs and risks of parenting

Most women give priority to their husbands' careers. This is so in even the most modern of marriages, even when women have great careers and even when they're making more money than their husbands. This prioritising of the man's career usually happens in a way that's never actually discussed between husband and wife. It's 5:30 pm and someone has to pick up the kids from childcare by 6:00 pm. It's the wife who leaves her work at the office half-finished. Both the wife and husband are in good jobs requiring travel. Somebody needs to stop travelling so much. It's she who downsizes her career.

You may assume that since you're being financially supported by your husband, you can downsize your career by switching to a less-demanding job, reducing your hours or even leaving the workforce for a few years. You may assume that someday when you choose to re-upsize your career, the working world will re-embrace you with open arms.

But such assumptions entail serious risks. Society is

not yet well-equipped to welcome you to downsize and upsize your career according to your timetable. When you subordinate your ambitions, there results a cascade of long-term consequences for your career and life. I see this every day as a headhunter watching women struggle with the consequences of these choices. Most women who downsize their careers will never catch back up. Their skills become outdated, their networks go stale, their jobs get filled up by ambitious others. Women rarely rejoin the workforce at anywhere near the level where they dropped off.

Parenting and career are totally different in their costs and benefits. When men support the family financially, they continue to receive recognition for their accomplishments. Their careers provide a source of enduring friendships and networks.

By contrast, women's tasks are neither financially nor socially remunerated. Stay-at-home moms across the board have low self-esteem and a low sense of personal competence, even in the realms of childcare and social skills. Being the mother to a young child is a major risk factor for depression. Motherhood itself is a major risk factor for poverty in a woman's old age. All this leads to a slow divergence of interests between many husbands and wives, in which they start to live in separate spheres.

Look around and see what happens to those who played by all the rules, marrying young and losing themselves in their roles as dutiful wives and mothers. They stop caring for themselves, stop giving themselves opportunities to grow and learn and be creative.

Many keep going in this mode for years, only to reach their forties and have their husbands abandon them for shiny younger women. It always gives me chills when I hear a man sum up the demise of an entire family history with those three awful little words, 'She got boring.'

Bearing and raising young children is the most vulnerable time in a woman's life. Marriage and children are clearly riskier for women than for men, since the costs of childcare, time, emotional energy, career opportunities and financial security are all borne by women.

The unspoken contract is that our husbands will share their future income with us and the kids. But as we see from all the studies, women who marry young have an excellent chance of divorcing young. And divorce results in grim financial prospects for mothers, even where the father is required to provide some financial support.

In China, after divorce, the father's wealth typically rises, while mother and child will have a much higher chance of being poor. Most women never get back on track financially, emotionally or spiritually. It's amazing that despite all this, 70 per cent to 80 per cent of divorces in China now are initiated by women, according to the Ministry of Civil Affairs.[2] This tells you how bad their marriages must have been.

Society calls us virtuous when we put our families ahead of our careers. 'So wonderful, sacrificing your career for your husband's!' It's no wonder that, although we praise parenting as the ultimate and most meaningful work, most men don't leap up to do it full-time.

It's taken me a long time to say this, because for most of my adult life I've defended the choices of my women friends who stayed home with the kids. I felt that women need to have choices, and having choices means that we should never be disparaged if we choose to focus on our kids. Politically and philosophically, I still believe this.

As a practical matter, though, I'm now convinced that being an exclusive caregiver to one's family is not a good choice for any woman. I look around at the lives of my peers who've focused all their energies on their families, and I see how nearly all have ended up lonely, bored, unfulfilled and ultimately, depressed. Many of these women are rich, so money is not the issue. Being rich does not dull the pain of not participating. My happiest friends are those who are somehow contributing to the outside world.

As women, we need identities outside of the home. This is important for our relationship with ourselves as well as for our relationship with others. And the best way to raise children who are independent is to show them what an independent woman looks like.

How can we allow women to both realise their own dreams and raise healthy families? In the speeding highways of modern-day careers, we need efficient on-ramps and off-ramps where both women and men can leave and re-enter the workforce in order to take care of other priorities such as raising kids or caring for elderly parents.

The world contains various examples of societies that pay men to spend two or four years in mandated military service. Bright minds could work out the details of creating a system for family leave for women and men. I believe that, if there's the will to create a similar system for women and families, it can be done.

Meanwhile, there's money to be made by companies that proactively leverage the huge workforce of underemployed mothers. Look no further than the great companies established by women entrepreneurs themselves after they became mothers.

Having it all means *not* doing it all

Some celebrities make it all look easy. Take Angelina Jolie. Box office queen, stunningly beautiful, married to one of the world's sexiest men, a global humanitarian and mother to six kids. How does she do it all?

Well, she doesn't, exactly. She reportedly doesn't allow her nannies to be photographed but she employs at least five of them, in addition to the teachers, house-cleaners and all the other personal staffers who make up Angelina Inc.

I respect Angelina. Her acting abilities are without question, and she manages her image more ferociously than anyone else in Hollywood. As a result of all this, she's one of the world's most powerful actresses. That said, when Angelina presents herself as ubermama, we do ourselves a disservice if we take away a feeling of inadequacy for not doing it all.

People sometimes ask me, 'How do you do it all?' Well, I don't. I have a fantastic husband, a live-in nanny who cares for our girls and cooks for us, and someone else who comes in to clean our house.

Nearly every major company CEO is a man. Their eighty-hour workweeks mean that they are not home raising the kids. They don't have to, because most have two important assets: A stay-at-home wife and lots of paid help.

Having a stay-at-home wife is indeed a fantastic asset. She loves your kids like herself. She maintains the household. She's there all the time. She even gives you sex.

But it's expensive. Salary.com pins the value of a stay-at-home mom at US $1,15,000 per year.[3] That's like a director or a junior vice president level at a small global company.

And household help is expensive, especially in the US. That means you have to make good money to pay for that help. And that means delaying kids until you're financially ready, both for their sake and for yours.

The way to have it all, to pursue your dreams, to be a great mother, to do it all, gracefully and well and without losing your sanity, is not to even try to do it all. Here is how to have it all: First, marry a man who will be a real partner to you. That right there will be a huge help. Next, surround yourself with all the other help you need. That could be in the form of your parents or in-laws or paid help or anyone else you can muster up.

For women today, marriage and motherhood confer significant benefits but significant costs and risks as well. A successful marriage does not require that everything be equal. It does mean that you and your future husband agree on the arrangements.

Society demands that we marry, and yet its dogma is of zero help after the wedding day is over. As a result, brides spend more time planning their weddings than planning for their marriages.

But planning ahead is crucial to your life, as Gloria Steinem counsels:

> Planning ahead is one of the most reliable measures of class. Rich people plan for several generations forward; poor people plan for Saturday night. By that measure, even women born into powerful families are often

lower class. They give control of their lives over to their husbands, children, community, society.[4]

Your dreams for a life of purpose and a life filled with love are necessary and essential to who you are. Do not give up your dreams for either an imagined life of luxury or for an idealised vision of maternal service. Our lives are fluid. Circumstances change. Life evolves. We evolve. If you want it all, you can have it all, but at every point along the way, visualise your options and plan ahead.

Chapter 5

Solitude and the Lost Art of Creativity

Every child is an artist. The problem is how to remain an artist once he grows up.

—Pablo Picasso

A less obvious way that society's marriage fantasy 'disserves' us is by instilling in us a fear of being alone. We start to equate being alone with being lonely and isolated. This may make you want to immediately run out and fill up your life with a man. Put aside this urge. Enjoy being single, because it's during your alone times that you build independence. The journey to self-knowledge is always a solitary one.

An emerging body of research finds that time alone is not simply a problem to be treated. On the contrary, time alone is crucial to our well-being. There's something very nourishing about being able to decompress at the end of a busy day and being able to establish some control over how we spend our time.

And as long as our time alone is by choice and isn't motivated by fear or social anxiety, solitude actually helps us develop empathy. Says University of Chicago psychologist John Cacioppo, 'You need to be able to recharge on your own sometimes. Part of being able to connect is being available to other people, and no one can do that without a break.'

Throughout the history of world cultures, solitude has long been associated with spirituality, creativity and strength. In the lyrical words of philosopher Zhou Guoping, 'Solitude is a beautiful moment and the wonderful experience of our lives. Although we are alone, we find fulfilment. Solitude is a necessary space for growing spirit and soul.'

Part of our fear of being alone comes from the fact that solitude doesn't come with an instruction manual. What should we do when we're alone? Zhou Guoping has the answer:

> In solitude, we withdraw from others and business and we retreat into ourselves. We face ourselves and God alone. We start a conversation with our souls and the mysterious higher power of the universe. Only in solitude do we start to live the lives of our soul.

Creativity flourishes in solitude, because it's only when we're alone that we reach inside and find the beauty in our deepest thoughts. My best photography, my best writing and in fact the best of anything I've ever created, was created in solitude.

Too often, solitude is lost in this era of hyper-connection, when everyone in the world is only an IM away, and when we're bombarded by the constant barrage of social media. Solitude gives us the tranquility to think and space to create and, through that creating, solitude allows us to discover ourselves.

What is creativity?

When Steve Jobs died, there was an outpouring of hand-wringing about how China or India will never produce its own Steve Jobs because today's Chinese and Indian lack creativity. I have a different view. I agree that the test-taking and memorisation culture has beaten down our innate creativity. But I disagree that this generation, therefore, is doomed. Because just as creativity can be lost, it can be found and nurtured, and in a much more powerful way when we're older, since as adults we have a better grasp of the tools—literal and figurative—for expressing our creativity.

Many of us think of creativity in a binary way, as if a person is either creative or she's not, creative people being special 'other' people, artists and musicians and a certain black-turtleneck-wearing technology executive who recently departed the Earth. That kind of mythology is nonsense. Creative people are not other people. Creative people are us, as soon as we start creating things. We can be creative at work or at play, when we're designing software, or starting a company, or developing a marketing strategy. We're being creative when we're doing any of those things in just the way that satisfies us.

It's easy to let inertia govern our lives. It's easy to

blindly proceed along the paths circumscribed by what we studied in school and what other people expect of us. Many of us don't get what we want out of life because we have no idea who we are or what we want.

You have a self buried deep inside that must find a way out. How do you find your voice? You find your voice when you create something that comes from inside, because that's when you focus yourself on thinking, feeling, discovering and dreaming. The act of creating something new forces you to have an interior dialogue with yourself, to listen to your inner voice.

And so, each act of creating is an act of discovering who you are. No creative outlet, no way to access and find your inner voice. That's why having a creative outlet is essential for your self-confidence and to your having a happy and well-rounded life. Lack of a creative outlet has been shown to trigger apathy, loneliness, stress and depression.

It makes me sad to think about what my life would be like now if I'd never developed any creative outlets. By now I'd be another sad and frustrated middle-aged woman.

One of the great researchers on creativity is the Hungarian psychologist Mihaly Csikszentmihalyi (pronounced 'chick-sent-me-high-ee'). He says:[1]

> Of all human activities, creativity comes closest to providing the fulfilment we all hope to get in our lives. Call it full-blast living. Creativity is a central source of meaning in our lives. Most of the things that are interesting, important and human are the result of creativity. What makes us different from apes—our language, values, artistic expression, scientific

understanding and technology—is the result of individual ingenuity that was recognised, rewarded and transmitted through learning. When we're creative, we feel we are living more fully than during the rest of life. The excitement of the artist at the easel or the scientist in the lab comes close to the ideal fulfilment we all hope to get from life, and so rarely do.

I have devoted thirty years of research on how creative people live and work, to make more understandable the mysterious process by which they come up with new ideas and new things. Creative individuals are remarkable for their ability to adapt to almost any situation and to make do with whatever is at hand to reach their goals. If I had to express in one word what makes their personalities different from others, it's complexity. They show tendencies of thought and action that in most people are segregated. They contain contradictory extremes; instead of being an 'individual,' each of them is a 'multitude.'

Creating creates complexity. It's a great way to broaden our perspectives, because doing so forces us to develop and draw from all our ideas and experiences.

Creative work requires risk-taking

By the time I was appointed deputy mayor, I'd worked hard to polish my English, so writing speeches became a terrific creative outlet. I wrote my own speeches. As a politician, I could say something in a straightforward way, 'Register for our new college financial-aid programme!' Or I could try to inspire someone. I would imagine a young mother in front of her TV, made cynical by the empty promises of politicians who'd come before. I tried to insert just the right golden words, the vivid illustrations, the pregnant pauses, to help her look beyond the daily obstacles and envision an educated tomorrow for her children.

After politics, I entered headhunting and my writing slowed to a trickle. My clients, busy CEOs and HR directors, had no interest in lyrical turns of phrase. Each time I assessed a candidate, my clients wanted to know one thing, 'Should I hire this person?' I limited my writing to serving their needs.

Those years, life was a whirl, a good whirl. Companies depended on me to make crucial decisions, such as who to hire as CEO. I spent a lot of time on airplanes, whisking from one city to the next. Life was glamorous, and I made more money than I'd ever made before. I got married and had my first baby.

But something seemed a bit amiss. Amidst the mad scramble of a big career, dating, marriage and family, I felt slightly off-balance. I was running so hard in my career and in my life, rushing from one thing to the next that I'd never had time—never made time—to be still and simply think.

Then I turned 40, known here in the States as 'midlife crisis' time. The stereotypical American male divorces his long-time wife (he married too young!), finds a much-younger doll to hang on his arm, and buys a Porsche to carry her around in. To me, such voguish midlife accessories held no appeal. For one thing, I'd only recently married Mr Right and didn't want a young boyfriend. And I'd already bought my hot sports car.

Headhunting was lucrative. No complaints there. But what I did miss from my days in public service was a way to make the world a better place. I missed helping people, on a large scale, in ways that were personal and important to them.

How could I contribute something meaningful?

As a headhunter, I was at the table as my clients hired ambitious young Asians at the entry levels and then consistently passed them over when announcing promotions. I noticed how so many of these young people could benefit from a little mentoring, and how they lacked any mentorship at all. I decided to start a careers blog, in Chinese and English, on the unspoken rules of getting to the top in global companies. I called it Global Rencai.

Shortly after starting the blog, I was contacted by a mysterious Beijing-based editor with an unusual single-word name: Tangtang. She wanted me to write a book for women. 'Sounds interesting,' I replied, 'but I don't want to alienate my male readers.' We emailed back and forth a few times, neither one convincing the other. Soon, she disappeared.

Life went on. Headhunting kept me busy. I had a second baby, a girl again. That got me thinking seriously about the world awaiting my future young women. Also, I noticed something odd happening with the blog. Men were reading it, but women were devouring it. Women were pushing it worldwide, across online forums I'd never even heard of. I realised that, yes, the blog had male readers, but it had female fanatics. In spite of me, Global Rencai had become a women's blog.

Then Tangtang reappeared, still wanting me to write a book for women. It would be a sensation, she was sure of it. I admired her persistence. And this time, I was ready to talk. To test the waters, I wrote and posted a piece called 'Do not marry before age 30'. Within hours, traffic spiked so high that my servers crashed.

So I took a sabbatical from headhunting to write the book. I wrote swiftly, the words pouring onto the screen. 'Do this, and then do that!' In my mind, the book was shaping up as a savvy instruction guide to life and men.

The first half was done in a snap. I was well ahead of deadline. 'Finally,' I thought, 'I've made it!' I had worked, *so hard,* for two decades, and I looked forward to summer and fall on Easy Street. A little of this, a little of that. Writing. Tennis. Travel. Chocolate bonbons.

Or so I thought. Until I showed my draft to Tangtang. She woke me from my daydreams. 'Oh no!' she exclaimed. 'Readers don't want a list of do's and don'ts! They need your stories! Write about when you felt vulnerable!'

When I felt vulnerable?

My breath left my body. This was not what I'd had in mind when I signed that book deal. After all, politics in America is a Darwinian sport, and we who survived did so by hiding our vulnerabilities. I'd spent twenty years burnishing an image as a superwoman who leaped from one tall building of success to the next. I was not keen to give all that up.

Did women even want my stories?

Time for another blog experiment. I wrote a piece about how through my twenties, I'd felt lost and insecure, and posted it. Traffic soared. Proving two things: (1) Why Tangtang makes the big bucks; and (2) I had to start over on the book. As they say here in Hollywood when a studio rejects a script: 'Re-write!'

I started writing this book all over again. The second time around has been a whole different process from the first. This time, I'm looking in the mirror, making note of all the blemishes that were sympathetically concealed in my recent spreads in *Rayli and Marie Claire China* (Their make-up artists and photographers are magicians).

Going well beyond the glossy magazine images, I feel as if I'm on an archaeological excavation of my innermost thoughts. Each day, I carefully brush away the sediment, uncover shards of ideas, and raise them to the light for examination. The ones which might prove useful I painstakingly articulate into physical form on the screen.

It's quiet in my office. The hours fly by. A book project that began as a springtime lark has shape-shifted into the hardest, most invigorating, most maddening, most personally satisfying thing I have ever done.

This is better than chocolate bonbons. After all, I want my two future young women to be brave, and I hope that someday they'll aspire to more than a comfortable life. So I'd better set them an example. The fact is, I'm too young to retire, and damn it, I want my work to matter.

If you're a woman, write every day

I've found writing to be a very special creative outlet. Writing is immediate and accessible. You don't need to buy any special equipment or to get any special training to start. If you can read, you can write.

Writing is different from photography. With photography, we can make choices with subject, composition, film speeds, shutter speeds, lens aperture and many other tricks in the darkroom, but essentially we're working with images. Writing, on the other hand, forces us to take the ideas in our head and make them understandable by transferring them into words on screen or paper. To write effectively requires a good vocabulary. Our brains need to be in constant brainstorming mode, rolling through all our available words to translate our ideas in just the right way.

An odd thing about writing is that before we sit down to write we don't have to know what we'll be writing about. I once read that a person asked his professor what he thought about a particular subject. The professor replied, 'I don't know, I haven't written about that yet.' I thought that was an odd thing to say until I started writing this book. I've since realised that writing is a remarkably powerful way to explore ideas, since thoughts are created in the act of writing.

If you have trouble asking for what you want or addressing tough situations, then writing will train you to structure words diplomatically to achieve your goals. Writing trains us to shape our messages and gives us the space to do so without anyone nearby. When we can structure our words in writing we can translate our skills into effective speaking.

The skill of communicating clearly, concisely and beautifully atrophies without practice. Particularly for those of us who've never learned to express our feelings effectively, writing gives us that training, teaching us the sound of our own voices and showing us how to express ourselves so we're understood. Keep your writing muscles in top shape for the benefit of your inner life, your social life and your professional life.

When I started writing this book I reviewed a few writers' blogs for tips. I liked this one: 'If you're a writer, write every day.' Since then, I've gained so much from writing that I want to revise that to, 'If you're a woman, write every day.' Even if it's just ten minutes a day, write. It will give you something to look forward to, a date with yourself. Some days you may stop after ten minutes. Other days, you may continue writing for thirty or even sixty minutes.

Writing gives us a built-in 'pause' button to process what's happened in our day and to plan our responses. By allowing the words to flow out of us, we find the thoughts we've been holding back as we cope with everyday life. Writing time is often the only time we consider the questions of our lives. Why am I on the path I'm on? Is it still the right path for me? Writing is when we face ourselves with honesty.

Writing is the one thing that I do wholly alone. It gives me the psychic space, a room, even if imaginary, to call my own. It gives me permission for solitude. I read somewhere that male authors start writing at age twenty, while female authors start writing at age forty. I can see why.

We women get so infernally busy that it feels like a delicious pleasure to simply sit still and think.

At this point, you may assume that I'm talking about journal writing. I know of many women who make journal writing an important part of their day. But what I've found is that writing anything that's creative, that comes from inside of me, gives me that 'pause' button I need for life. It's the act of writing that calls forth my inner dialogue.

Each time we write, our voices become clearer, more focused and stronger, until soon our writing is inseparable from our speaking voices. As we strengthen our voices, they show up in other parts of our lives as well. In this way, writing helps us develop voices that are natural, strong and confident.

To reach your potential, you need flow

Have you ever been so absorbed in your work that you lost track of time? It happened to me in my high school darkroom, and it happens to me now when I write. This state is called 'flow', an important concept whose father is, again, Dr Csikszentmihalyi, who's a psychologist but he's also an anthropologist, philosopher and a real Renaissance man.

Dr Csikszentmihalyi and his colleagues have studied flow in over 10,000 people across many cultures—tapestry-weaving women in Borneo, meditating monks in Europe, and many others.

They all say the same thing, that being in a state of flow feels like being carried spontaneously and effortlessly by a current.

He describes flow as an optimal state of consciousness, when people feel 'strong, alert, in effortless control, unselfconscious and at the peak of their abilities.'[2] It's when you're stretching your abilities and when you're primed to learn new things, to become better at what you're doing, to invent new things and to discover new things.

When you achieve flow, worries fall away and are

replaced by a sense of bliss. The conscious part of you switches off; your awareness of yourself slips away. You forget yourself as an entity altogether. And you just do. You're completely immersed in what you're doing, and you're just moving along with the logic of the activity.

As human beings, to be happy, we must stretch ourselves, to challenge ourselves in projects that use us fully and well. People who achieve flow are challenging themselves and creating their best work. To be a high-performer, you need to achieve flow somewhere in your life. If you don't have an activity in your life in which you're regularly achieving flow, then you're not reaching the peak of your potential.

To achieve flow:

- You must have solitude so that you can work without interruptions.
- Your skills must be stretched but not overwhelmed. Your work is not too hard, but hard enough to really challenge you and make you grow and learn.
- You must already have some experience with the task, so that you can keep working as the conscious part of you switches off.
- You must be doing something that's intrinsically rewarding to you, that you want to do and that springs forth from within you.
- You must have autonomy and be able to complete the task in just the way that satisfies you. In this task, you must be your own boss.

Sound familiar? That's right. The best way to achieve flow is to immerse yourself in a creative outlet. I don't know much about ancient philosophies, but it seems to me that the concept of solitude resembles Qingjing (tranquility), and creative flow sounds like Wúwéi (effortless action). Being in a state of solitude and using this time to achieve creative flow can infuse our lives with a sense of peace and tranquility and help us to focus on excelling in all of life's important priorities.

Your turn

Many of you have been my loyal readers for some time, starting with my blog and now with this book. But creativity is not a spectator sport.

You may feel as if you've spent so many years smothered under all the pressure that you don't even recognise the sound of your own voice. This is the time in your life to rid yourself of all the static and tune in to that inner voice. At first, you may feel that your inner voice has a really weak signal, small, scratchy, shaky and hard to hear. It may not be loud and confident. But each time you're still and pay it attention and let it guide you, it will gain power. If you don't have a creative outlet, write.

Create something, make it beautiful and add to it every day in just the way that satisfies you. Creativity is habit-forming. Revel in the way it feels when you've created something especially great.

As you continue to create new things, your creative work will centre you and strengthen you. You'll find your creativity beginning to flourish. Ideas will pop up from out of nowhere. You'll find inspiration in big and little things. You'll find yourself connecting ideas in other areas of your life outside of your creative endeavour. By the way, creative people need more sleep, so get your eight hours of sleep a night!

Part of the fun is that you don't have to express yourself perfectly clearly. Your expression can be loud and public, or subtle and abstract, a delicious little innuendo that only you know. Creating something is the best antidote for anytime you're feeling lonely or powerless, confused, bored, uninspired or sad.

Each time you create something, you're making a stand for yourself. Your sovereign act of creation is a statement about who you are, what you feel and what you think is important. It's a statement of your sovereignty as a human being.

Chapter 6

Be True to Yourself

What matters is not what you can do, but what you should do.
—Jack Ma

The malaise of insecurity that ails women is not limited to those in their twenties and thirties. Older women often have it even worse. Here's what I'm hearing:

> 'For years I've tried to keep my husband happy, but I think he's getting some action on the side. The thought of him with another woman sickens me. My life is sliding away.'
>
> 'I feel trapped in a life I never planned. I work around the clock for my boss, my husband, my children. I've lost touch with who I am.'

Do you know a woman who *doesn't* overgive?

The cheeky blog *StuffWhitePeopleLike.com* includes 'Asian girls' because 'Asian women avoid key white women characteristics such as having a midlife crisis, divorce and hobbies that don't involve taking care of the children.'

How sad! Midlife crisis and divorce are not events to aspire to, and yet after thousands of years, women are so accustomed to devotion to those around us that it's hard to rid ourselves of the mentality of dutiful servant even as we yearn for more.

Now, we expect of ourselves perfect performance in multiple roles: Gorgeous woman, dutiful daughter, adoring wife, angelic mother. It's no wonder that in the rush to meet all these expectations, many of us lose our own selves.

We each got to where we are now by learning to excel at doing as we're told, deflecting attention from ourselves. Many of us have gotten so used to not talking about what we want that we don't even know anymore who we are or what we want.

On one hand, we feel, 'Being a good woman means that I focus on other people's needs.' On the other hand, we feel, 'I want and deserve a man who will cherish and care for me.' This puts us in a state of constant tension. Until we recognise that we're worthy of love, we'll not get the love we need.

I know a woman who's like a male-magnet, but for precisely the wrong men—boyfriends and bosses who treat her like dirt. Her nice-girl approach undermines not just her self-confidence but also her ability to have a real relationship with a man. Maybe you know her too; maybe you are her.

You are responsible for the people around you, because the people you attract are those who reinforce how you feel about yourself. There's a difference between giving to others—a good thing—and having your identity so wrapped up around the 'good woman' role that you chronically deny your own needs.

When we build our lives around overextending ourselves and sacrificing our own needs to help others we inevitably create lives of exhaustion, frustration and feelings of failure. Uber-caregivers whose identities are based on being in this unnatural state, pay a very high price indeed, because burnout is a form of self-abuse. It's truly depressing when you think about how so many women live such broken lives, for the simple reason that all their lives they've simply just tried to be what our society trains us to be good women.

We face so much pressure to conform and be measured against other people that we've beaten out of ourselves the expectation that our lives should be filled with joy. Why should we not expect to have joy in our lives? Why should we not receive the love of a good man? I was struck by this quote from Gloria Steinem's book *Doing Sixty and Seventy*:

> I have yet to meet a woman who has completely kicked the habit of leading a derived life that depends more on her sense of others than her sense of herself. Even if we've refused to be hyper-responsible for the welfare of a family, we often feel too responsible for what goes on at work. Even if we're no longer trying to surgically implant our ego into the body of a husband or children, we still may be overly dependent on being needed—by co-workers and bosses, lovers and friends, even by the very [political] movements that were intended to free us from all that.

When I first read this quote I thought, 'Wow!' Even our feminist icons have struggled with giving too much. As I look back, I see that every time I've felt lost or stuck is when I've momentarily set myself aside in service to someone else's expectations—my parents, a boyfriend, a company I worked for.

It's a requirement of daily life to put others' needs before ours at times. Many nights, my body has begged to collapse in bed and instead, I've had to stay awake to feed my baby. But many of us find it hard to ever say no to other people's requests, even when those requests are unreasonable. If someone asks us to do something within our power, our immediate response is, 'Sure, I can do that!'

Until we actively acknowledge ourselves as worthy and deserving of our own care, we'll never achieve the balance that we crave. We need to set boundaries with the people in our lives. To stop living our lives by simply responding to the demands of others. To acknowledge their feelings, let them know we value the relationship, and that while we can't meet their every need, we hope they'll find it helpful what we are able to offer.

We can each start to care for ourselves by simply committing to treat ourselves as well as we treat others. Does that seem like too much to ask?

For many of us, the biggest pressure to abandon our dreams comes not from our mothers, but from our mothers-in-law. Mothers-in-law who demand that we abandon our own selves and devote our lives to serving their sons and grandchildren. That's why I feel especially lucky that when we married, Dave's parents embraced me not just as a daughter-in-law but as a woman. Dave's mother, Lennie, herself has masterfully and gracefully combined multiple roles as teacher, community leader and mother throughout her life, and has been a continuing source of advice for me on how to have it all.

You might assume that since I didn't have babies until after having enjoyed a wonderful career I'd have been immune to the women's malady of burnout. And yet, both times after I gave birth, I fell into a stupor of overwork. The person who woke me up was Lennie, who saw me one day, tired and haggard, and admonished me to make time for myself. She pushed me towards tennis, a sport to which I was first introduced by Dave, and which I now commit to playing regularly. Tennis makes me feel fit and strong, and I love that feeling. Now, tennis is me-time.

Learn to say no

A strong woman is a woman who knows how to say 'no'. There's a great *New Yorker* magazine cartoon showing a man in his office looking at his calendar and saying into the telephone, 'No, Thursday's out. How about never—is never good for you?' I know a lot of strong women, but I don't think I know any woman who says no quite so emphatically. That's because saying no goes against everything we as women have ever been taught to do, which is to say 'yes'.

The first thing we must say no to is any form of abuse in our lives. Since burnout is a form of self-abuse, we need to say no to burnout.

And we must say no to abuse by others. As I write this, the ongoing drama of Crazy English founder Li Yang's divorce from Kim Lee continues to reverberate in a remarkable public discussion of domestic violence and whether and how it's tied to our Asian culture.

When we think of abuse, we often think of those horrible news stories and Weibo or Facebook photos of women who've been physically disfigured by abuse. But not all abuse is physical. Emotional abuse can be just as destructive, and even more confusing to understand.

Often the hardest step in getting away from abuse is recognising when a relationship is abusive. After all, you can't address a problem you don't know is there. That's why it's so useful that in his book *The New Rules of Marriage,* best selling author and psychologist Dr Terrence Real defines abuse:

- Yelling and screaming
- Name-calling: Any sentence that begins with 'You are a G'.
- Shaming or humiliating: Communicating that someone is a bad or worthless person. Ridiculing someone, mocking, being sarcastic, humouring or being patronising.
- Telling another adult what she should do, or how she should think or feel.
- Making promises and breaking them
- Lying or manipulating: Deliberately falsifying information or dishonestly changing your behaviour in an attempt to control your partner, for example: 'Don't worry about me. I'll be fine out here in the rain. You go have a good time.'

What makes abuse so confusing is that most abusers are not like the evil bad guys that we see in the movies.

Abusers are human too, which means that at times, they show kindness and generosity. Usually they don't even know they're being abusive. In their minds, they're the victims, misunderstood and under attack, and their abusive behaviour is only a response to a provocation. Many abusers lack the basic emotional skills necessary to be competent adults with functional relationships.

But just because abusers don't recognise their abusive behaviour does not make their abusive behaviour any less dangerous to those who try to love them. When we ignore or cover up abuse, it doesn't go away. It escalates. And when children are present, abuse has cascading effects on future generations, since children who grow up witnessing abuse become perpetrators and victims of abuse as adults.

There is absolutely no reason that abuse should be a part of your life. There are plenty of good men and women in this world who do not perpetrate or condone abuse. Do not date or marry someone who abuses you. If you are married to someone who abuses you, seek help right away for yourself and your family. You can and must demand that your family be healthy.

And because we choose not to live in a society governed by abuse, let's not tolerate abuse when it's directed at our sisters, brothers, friends or colleagues. For us all to say no to abuse would be for us to step out of women's traditionally passive role and stop the legacy of abuse in society. Because we're making culture now, too. And the culture we create will be based on dignity and mutual respect. If together we all link arms to say no to abuse, then in a generation's time, no one will be able to say that abuse is a normal part of Asian culture anymore.

How to be true to yourself

I'm blessed to count among my friends many powerful women. Here's what they look like:

- They're joyful, strong and self-assured.
- No matter the number of roles they play—career woman, mother, etc.—they seem to gracefully excel at them all and still make time for their friends.
- They're at peace with the choices they've made, they feel their lives are on track now and they're excited about their futures.
- They're growing and learning every day. They're constantly reinventing themselves.
- They exert a centripetal pull in the universe, attracting people from all directions. They're popular and influential. This leads to good things and even more opportunities in their lives.

What they do have in common is not a trait but a practice. Each approaches her life from the standpoint of what is true to her. For women today, giving ourselves permission to be true to ourselves is life's most important lesson and also life's hardest. After all, the last thing we would want is to be called selfish!

But when we're constantly overworked and overstressed from the strain of trying to be all things to all people, we serve no one well. The reason it's so hard to be true to ourselves is that, as women, we're taught to be true to everyone but ourselves.

Faced with a world that expects so much of us, but that is blind to who we are and what we need, how can we learn to be true to ourselves? To figure that out for yourself, quiet down all the noise and tune in to your inner voice.

- **Identify those moments in your life when your heart sings.** Recall a moment in the past year when your heart sang. When you felt strong, in charge, happy, and you were so involved in what you were doing that time just flew by. What were you doing? Where were you? Who were you with? Picture yourself again in this moment, in as much vivid detail as you can. As you think about it, you may feel yourself relax. Your breathing may slow down. You might even smile to yourself. This is, in fact, an exercise to help you identify your natural strengths and passions.
- **Commit to making more of those moments in your life.** What are the elements of your role as a daughter, girlfriend, career woman, wife, mother, that bring you joy? Start to create more of these moments in your life. Reorganise your life and your career to focus on doing more of those things. As you prioritise those things, move other activities off of your to-do list.

In the 1970s, as economic growth slowed in industrialised countries, companies realised they couldn't do everything. They had to make choices and they needed a way to think about those choices. Corporate strategy took off as a management discipline. But what Harvard Business School professors Clark Gilbert and Joseph Bower find is that, for companies, corporate strategy is not enough.[1] Companies routinely plan to do one thing and then actually do another. The problem lies in the reality of how resources are allocated across company operations.

As an example, take the case of how one US newspaper

company has failed to adapt quickly enough to the internet. Years ago, its Board and CEO decided to shift its priorities away from print and towards the internet. However, at the operating level, an advertising sales representative said to himself, 'I can sell a US $40,000 newspaper display ad to my usual customers, or I can go out and try to find a new customer and sell them a US $2,000 internet banner ad.' Each day, he came to work and continued to do things the old way, allocating his time and attention to selling print ads to his usual customers.

Taken together, the millions of resource allocation decisions made every day by that sales representative and thousands of his colleagues have prevented the company from shifting its operations over to the internet according to company strategy. As a result, the company has gone downhill fast, and now is struggling financially.

In my life, I face exactly the same problem that a company does. I have a bunch of priorities that compete for my resources. I'm trying to shape a better world, have a great career, be a good wife, raise terrific little girls, learn and grow through new ideas and experiences, care for my friends, stay healthy and fit and so on. I have a finite amount of time and energy. I may say that I have a certain set of priorities, but whether I succeed depends on how much of my resources I actually allocate to any one of those priorities.

To me, crossing forty means that life no longer feels as if it will stretch on forever. I think back to all the times I've mistakenly allocated my resources, for example, by focusing too much time and attention on boyfriends who now are unimportant to me. All that time is now irretrievable.

When I was younger, I always thought that life was someplace else, and I was working towards it. I've since realised that the future is right now. My most precious resource is time, and I'm trying to be deliberate in how I allocate it. Each hour that I fritter away, mindlessly checking social media or watching TV, is an hour I'll never get back. I've stopped carrying on as if my whole life is ahead of me, because it no longer is.

You might think that crossing into midlife is saddening but for me it's been greatly liberating. The best part of growing up is gaining perspective, and now I'm committed to being true to myself by focusing on the people and the priorities which matter to me most.

And so, to help answer the question of how to be true to ourselves, I find useful the MBA framework of resource allocation. Joy comes from understanding what matters to me, and then living my life to reflect that commitment.

Other people sometimes question the choices I make. Sometimes their motivations are selfish. They feel that my choices are not the best ones for their lives. Other times, they disagree that I've made the right choices for my life. But I've found that in order to achieve anything at all, one must be willing to disappoint some people.

Perhaps, especially because I've led a higher-profile life, people are always making demands on my time. They want help in reaching their goals, and my name pops up into the mind as someone who might be able to help. I could have two full-time jobs doing nothing but providing free individualised career counselling to all the job seekers who ask me for it. My writing is my way to help them and still be able to work towards my own priorities.

But some people will never be satisfied. No matter how much you give them, they always want more. Often, those who make the most unreasonable requests are those who are most lost in their own lives. If you keep satisfying other people's unreasonable demands, they'll keep asking for more. Say no, and they'll learn to treat you with more respect. We teach people how to treat us.

Others will love you more

When we incorporate effective resource allocation into our lives the following things happen:

- We have more time in our lives because we're focused on doing fewer things and doing those well.
- We have more purpose in our lives because we're focused on certain things rather than trying to please everyone.
- Our lives feel more balanced because each area of our lives gives us strength rather than sap it.
- We're able to do more for others, because by addressing our own needs we're gaining the strength we need to help others.

Don't worry too much about big questions like 'Who am I?' and instead allocate your resources every day towards what's most important to you.

Act boldly. It's one thing to know what you need to do and another to act upon it. Learn to trust your heart, and you'll be compelled to make large and small changes in your life. You may need to negotiate with your boss a shift in your responsibilities. You may need to let go of relationships that pull you down.

Effective resource allocation becomes habit forming. The paradoxical thing about our becoming more self-centred women is that people love us more. When we remain true to ourselves we attract people, women and men, who want to be near us for who we really are.

I see more clearly now the tyranny of simply living one's life by doing what's expected. By letting go of society's rules, I feel as if I've emerged into my own person, a butterfly emerging from its chrysalis. I cherish the freedom to be myself, simply and joyously, without apologies and explanations.

Being true to yourself is a powerful aphrodisiac to a good man—the type of man who wants a true partner, who will deserve and honour you. Dave in his early forties was busy with the standard early-forties, nice-looking-guy routine of dating a rotation of pretty young girls. But then we met, and then, as he puts it, he quickly 'cleared out the stable'.

And then it was just me and him.

When you're a sexy mature woman who has it all together, and you're ready to pounce on a man of quality, the pretty young dolls don't stand a chance.

Chapter 7

Explore the Vast Possibilities of Your Life

Those who grow the fastest are the most curious, who absorb new knowledge like sponges. That's intellectual curiosity, which drives us to learn and explore new things.

—Zhang Xin

If you're single, don't take your singlehood for granted. Being single is an important time. This is your time, to find your voice and pursue your dreams in a way that's just not possible when you're with a partner.

If you think that later you'll have more time and energy to focus on yourself, forget it. From here on, life will only get more demanding. These are precious moments when you've left your family but not yet committed to a new family. Soon you may enter new long-term obligations that circumscribe your life forever.

Relish your fleeting freedom

Now is when you get to go out and do whatever you like. What will you have for dinner? Should you switch jobs? Should you date someone new? Should you buy that ridiculously expensive pair of shoes? Never again will you be able to make all these decisions completely on your own. These years are the only time that you'll ever get to experiment, stretch, live, love, laugh all by yourself.

This is the only time in your entire life that you'll get to be a little selfish and focus just on you, so don't fritter it away moping at home or yearning to be in a couple.

Grant yourself these years to wander around a bit in the world and explore the vast possibilities of your life. Being single can be the best years of your life—certainly the funniest and most fabulous and the time of greatest growth and learning. Make decisions based on the information you have and don't second-guess yourself. At this point, no doors have been firmly closed. Every possibility for your future is still open. Say yes to the unknown.

Freedom is a great reward for being on your own. And freedom, philosophers tell us, is a prerequisite to spiritual development. So take advantage of this special time to define who you are, what you're about and how you're different from everyone else. Spread your wings and fly towards self-discovery.

When you're single and unattached, focus on your career. Don't let your career be guided simply by what you've studied in the past, or by peer pressure, or by what your parents' friends kids are doing successfully, and don't hold yourself back waiting for marriage and motherhood.

Follow your heart in choosing one job over another, or in simply focusing your job around the things you like best.

My slow start in my first career

During my early years in LA, the employer I coveted most was Maguire Thomas Partners, at the time the most innovative, best financed, most risk-taking, most glamorous real estate development firm in the US.

Maguire was famous for having built the tallest office buildings on the West Coast. I don't even need to go into the phallic nature of contests to build the world's tallest office buildings; the imagery speaks for itself. This was the firm of the biggest of the big guys. I badly wanted to work for them. But I was a nobody, the firm did not offer internships, and there was no internet to help get me in the door. Also, there was a small problem that, despite the fact that I wanted to get into a profession full of men, I was clueless with men. I had to learn fast.

At first, I didn't know where to turn. Then, through research, I discovered that two of the firm's senior partners were on the board of directors of the USC Architectural Guild, the fundraising charity of the USC Architecture School. That would be my back door to the firm. I couldn't afford to go to the fancy fundraising events, but I could volunteer my time. I carved out around ten hours a week for this work. Those days, there was no such thing as email, so each event required lots of menial labour, stuffing envelopes, licking stamps, arranging chairs, etc. I did it all, and all for free. My work behind the scenes ensured that the events were beautiful and flawless, and that made those VIPs look good in front of the people they cared about most.

Well, those VIPs were no dummies, and so after a few months they appointed me an official committee member for upcoming events. Then after I'd volunteered in this way for two years, they appointed me to the charity's full board of directors. People were amazed, wondering, how did a young Chinese girl get on the board of such a prestigious charity? She must be rich!

By then, I'd earned the trust of the Maguire executives on the board, and it was simple for me to ask if there was anything I could help out with around the firm.

That's how I got my first dream job, as a project assistant with the firm. To many, it probably didn't look like a dream job. I was the only woman employee who wasn't a secretary, and my salary was less than half of what the secretaries were making. But I was thrilled.

Looking back, if I were to grade myself as a developer, I'd give myself an A minus. That's a confusing place to be, because I could work hard and make pretty good money. Over time as my career grew in the industry, the money I made was probably in the top few per cent of women my age in America. I know now that real estate was not a great fit for me, but I didn't know it then because the business was all I knew, and therefore I felt locked in.

Now, some might say that I wasted an entire decade in slavish work and two graduate degrees on a real estate career that I've since abandoned. But I view those years as far from a waste of time. That's because what I took away was not the thousands of hours spent mapping out sidewalk widths and projecting cash flows. Most valuable to my future were the soft skills I developed:

- The self-assurance that comes from forging your own path.
- How powerful people communicate with one another.
- How to accumulate knowledge from many different sources (structural engineering, architectural design, financing, politics) and assemble them into a coherent view of a problem.
- How not to be dejected by the here and now (a hardscrabble piece of dirt), but to boldly envision and focus on the future.
- How to develop a message and sell it.
- How to brand yourself so the relevant exciting people want to be with you.
- How to really connect with other people.

All these skills were key to my personal growth and led directly to my later appointment as deputy mayor. And it was because I was so alive and excited about my path that I was open to soaking in all this learning. In hindsight, my twenties were extraordinarily productive, just not in the way I intended.

Later when I was in public office, I'd lie awake nights wondering what to do with my career after politics. I was still fixated on real estate development, but the question was at which firm, and in what capacity?

Near the end of our four-year term, I confidentially contacted a headhunter at Heidrick & Struggles, the global executive search firm. We went to breakfast.

Me: 'It's time. I'm ready to come back to real estate.'

Him: 'You're leaving a high-profile position at a

relatively young age. People are watching. You'll want to make sure your next move is really successful.'

Me: 'Isn't that why we're meeting?'

Him: 'So you'll want to make sure that you choose a career path that will make you really successful.'

Uh-oh. This conversation was starting to make me nervous.

Me: 'Am I not a great developer? Do I not have two graduate degrees in this area?'

Him: 'Joy, you're a good developer. But, to be honest, there are developers, even right here in Los Angeles, who are stronger than you. I'm your friend and I want to see you succeed. You should focus on your true strengths.'

Oh God. I saw my life flash before my eyes. I was only thirty-five. Had my career already peaked? Was this the start of the long slow decline of my career, and my life?

Me: 'I thought my true strength was real estate development.'

Him: 'What I see is that you connect with people. You can talk with a CEO, you can talk with a homeless person. You are generous. You instinctively sense what it is people need, and you find a way to give it to them. You connect ideas in novel ways. You do these things better than anyone.'

Me: 'What does all this mean for my career? You think I should get into marketing?'

Him: 'No. I think of marketing as one-to-many messaging. Your skills are more personal, one-to-one. I think you should seriously consider a career in executive search. And I want to introduce you to our firm.'

After another eight months of meetings with the firm, and considering other options as well, I joined Heidrick & Struggles.

What are *your* A plus skills?

As I look back, those A plus skills that he identified have indeed been the key skills that made me successful both as a civic leader and as a headhunter. It's telling that, when I was a real estate developer, the media showed little interest in interviewing me. Any mark I've left on the world so far has been in my later work.

When I was a developer, work was work and play was play. I am more joyful now because now my work is an extension of who I am and while work is challenging, it is also a form of self-expression. Now the lines between work and play are blurred.

What are your A plus skills? What comes to you so naturally that when you are doing it, you're achieving flow, and it feels like you're just revelling in life on Earth?

I was lucky to have a headhunter come along and accurately sum up my A plus skills. When he did so, my first reaction was confusion. Yes, I thought, I love throwing parties and connecting interesting people. But that's not work! I couldn't believe that 'connecting with people' and 'connecting ideas' could even be considered skills.

Skills were things like Latin or finance that were hard and had to be learned.

As Asians, we're accustomed to working hard and to hardship. So it's easy to assume that work should be hard. It's counter-intuitive that work should be so easy as to feel completely natural.

Here's what I've concluded: Yes, work should be hard. To achieve flow, we need to challenge ourselves at the outer edge of our capabilities. But the type of work we choose should be work that is based around our natural A plus skills.

All those super successful people I've met over the years? They're not superhuman. If you sit down and evaluate them, as I do as a headhunter, you'll see they're not A plus in all areas. They're just A plus in the specific skills that are key to the careers they've chosen.

For your career to fulfil you, you need to use your strengths and you need meaning in your life. Israeli teacher Tal Ben-Shahar writes that when he graduated from college his philosophy professor said this to him, 'Life is short. In choosing a path, make sure you first identify those things that you can do well. Out of those, select the ones you want to do. Then, reduce your choice further by zooming in on what you really want to do. Finally, select those things that you really, really want to do—and then do them.'[1]

One thing that constantly amazes me as a headhunter is how special and unique each individual is. Two candidates can have nearly identical resumes and yet will be completely different when I meet them in person. We're all different in what skills we bring to the world and in how we find the meaning we need.

Don't get serious about your career until age forty

Your career will be made not in the next two years, but over the next half-century. Over that time, you'll have good jobs and bad jobs, good bosses and bad bosses. Your strengths will unfold over time as you develop them.

Don't stress about finding the perfect job right now. Give yourself permission to bounce around and explore different avenues. Much more important than any one choice you make in your career is how you learn and grow every single day in whatever it is that you are doing.

It's unrealistic to think that during your twenties you'll find the perfectly fulfilling job, because college doesn't prepare you with the skills and experience you need to succeed. So don't expect to find the perfectly fulfilling job in your twenties and don't expect to become an instant millionaire. You can expect a few years of seeming drudgery doing the menial things that the important people don't want to do.

Look at every job as an opportunity to learn in a new place and from new people. Sometimes you can learn even more from badly run companies and bad bosses than you can from good workplaces. Utilise this time to listen, observe and practice how to think strategically and how to work well with those around you. If you learn intently every day, you'll only fail upward.

By the way, a great job also provides you ready access to great men. Many women spend time agonising over every career change and yet sail almost at random into long-term boyfriend relationships. The fact is, for most of you, the only serious, life-altering mistake available during your twenties, the consequences of which can wreck your life, is your marriage choice. So relax about your career decisions and worry about not failing at the big one.

I know how it feels to struggle with too many choices. In this regard, the best advice that I've received came from former LA Mayor Richard Riordan. Mayor Riordan is a self-made centi-millionaire and a wise man who has reinvented himself multiple times. He said, 'Relax! You don't have to get serious about business till you turn forty!'

At first, Mayor Riordan's advice confused me. I considered forty old, too old, perhaps, to finally find one's true calling. Now, as a headhunter on the other side of forty, I realise there was a trick embedded in his words.

Yue-Sai Kan. Honghuang. Bill Gates. Oprah. The people who are most consistently successful over time are those who constantly stretch themselves until the age of forty. And by then, they're so accustomed to reinventing themselves that they keep going. They become so agile, so mature, so strong, that no matter how the world changes, they remain on top. They continue to change our world.

Living as we are at the chaotic start of the twenty-first century, we'll all continue to be confronted with a vast array of choices throughout our lives. Chances are, over the course of your life, you'll not only have multiple jobs, but multiple careers, as I've had. Even if you stay in one career your entire life, that one career will be profoundly different in a decade than it is now.

That means we all will have to keep reinventing ourselves, over and over again, throughout our lives. Canadian hockey player Wayne Gretzky, in spite of his mediocre stature, strength and speed, became the best hockey player in history on the strength of his intelligence and ability to read the game. In his famous words, 'A good hockey player plays where the puck is. A great hockey player plays where the puck is going to be.'

Every day, every year, consider how the world is changing and focus on developing yourself in order to thrive in that new world. Because in the course of 'finding' your career, what you're really doing is 'creating' a stronger, smarter, wiser, maturer, better you. You find yourself by creating yourself.

In my experience, the hard work of creating yourself can be greatly speeded by mentorship by others older and wiser. Yue-Sai, Maureen and the guys at Maguire Thomas Partners all were terrifically important to me through the strength of their own examples of how to live and work. I learned directly from their advice, but also indirectly by simply being with them.

To be your mentor, someone need not be enormously powerful or distinctive. She (or he) just needs to be someone from whom you can learn, and in fact, you can learn from everyone. How do you cultivate a mentor? I'm reminded of the wise words of a close friend, Joel Kurtzman, who is one of the world's top business strategists and a former editor-in-chief of the *Harvard Business Review*. Joel says that most highly successful people have been blessed with mentors, and that the way to develop someone as a mentor is to become his or her 'indispensable assistant'.

That's actually how I became close to each of my mentors. When you find someone you'd like to have as a mentor, don't approach her as a supplicant. 'Will you be my mentor?' Rather, approach her as someone with something to offer. Consider her goals, identify some things which she needs done and which you can do reliably and well, and offer to do them. For free. The free part is important, because if you ask for money, you're just becoming an employee. And what you're hoping to gain from this person is far more valuable to you than money.

Meanwhile, study remarkable people from afar. In this respect, the internet is an incredible resource which did not exist when I was starting out. Many outstanding people mentor millions virtually. Have you ever read a blog post or a Weibo quote and felt a spark of illumination? Such brief points of interaction can be as influential as spending hours with a personal mentor.

I spend time every day on the internet, following and learning from wonderful thinkers, philanthropists and others who are changing the world. In this way, I have developed many online mentors whom I've never met in person.

Go easy on yourself. This letter from the sixteenth century Roman Catholic Saint Francis de Sales which, five centuries later, rings truer now than ever:

> My dear,
>
> Have patience with all things, but chiefly have patience with yourself. Do not lose courage in considering your own imperfections but instantly set about remedying them—every day begin the task anew. Whatever your

task, begin every single day as if it's your first day battling this task ahead of you. Don't tell yourself that you've done it for however many days now so maybe just for today you can relax. No! Begin every day anew. Every day is your first day.

And remember, be patient. You will fail more than once. Be patient.

Truly yours,
Saint Francis de Sales

Work hard on things you're passionate about. It's through work that you'll discover your passions and that you'll develop a greater understanding, love and respect for yourself. Become a contender in the world of work, and you'll find that it's fun to achieve. And you'll find that nothing is quite as much fun as achieving at work that matters.

Dream big. You are neither average nor ordinary, so don't go for a life which is either average or ordinary. Become more than you think you are, more than you've been told you can be. Make every day an adventure.

Let nothing impede your dreams. Reach into the deepest part of yourself and meet life's challenges with grace and joy. Pursue your dreams and don't let anyone question your choices. Defy gravity and fly.

Then dazzle them with a flirty wink and a smile.

Chapter 8

The Power of Perspective

Imagination is more important than knowledge.

—Albert Einstein

All those years when I was struggling with English, my best was never good enough for me. I kept saying the wrong things at the wrong time, or the right things at the wrong time. And there I'd stand, helpless and exposed, thinking over and over again, God! What a stupid thing to say! I am such an idiot! For days, I'd replay that over and over again, in my head.

Everywhere I looked, someone was better than me. Look at him with the silver tongue! Why am I not graceful like that? That girl is a wizard on the financials. How can I compete? No matter how well I did something there was always a little voice picking at the chinks in my performance. If 100 people praised me for my work while three people criticised me, I'd focus on the criticisms. I was my own worst enemy.

Psychologists call this 'ruminating' and say that women are more prone to this habit than men. I believe that. When I see news reports of breathtakingly brazen sex scandals and financial scandals, the perpetrators are rarely women. Why? To start with, women rarely are breathtakingly brazen. We're always self-correcting. We would never want to embarrass ourselves or our families.

And that's a good thing. At the same time, we need to avoid being so self-correcting that we stab ourselves to death over minor mistakes that others don't even notice or remember.

Let's stop being our own worst enemies and start being our own best friends. That means being kind to ourselves, and celebrating our own growth and the daily victories that come along the way.

The competition for money and power

I grew up during the 1980s, the years known in America as the 'decade of greed'. The US economy was flying high, and consumers' tastes in 'adult toys'—cars, sailboats, LV handbags, etc.—ran towards conspicuous excess. Buttons and T-shirts sported the motto of the day: 'He who dies with the most toys, wins.'

Being a highly observant young student of life and lacking an internally driven sense of self-worth, I began to crave the outward signs of power and success. Over time, how I felt about myself was based on how I measured up against other people. Other extremely successful people.

Take Bill Gates. By the time I graduated from college, Bill Gates already had dropped out of college, built Microsoft and become a billionaire. He and I even had a slight personal connection, since his wife Melinda graduated from Duke the year I started there. Every time I read about Bill Gates, I felt a stab of anxiety. In contrast to them, I didn't know how I'd make my first million.

Then, there was my UCLA business school classmate who, upon our graduation, moved to Silicon Valley and rented out her garage to a couple of young kids. Right there, they started a search-engine company, and called it Google. She created their original doodles and became one of the company's first executives.

Lacking an independent road map, I measured myself by the exceptional people around me. Anytime I read news of someone, I wondered, why is this person ahead of me? What title does she have? And then, am I on the right track? Have I made a mistake somewhere?

Newspapers compounded my misery by printing the ages of all those successful people right beside their names. When someone was my age or younger, I felt nauseous. Where did I go wrong?

Did all that bellyaching serve me any good? Does competition motivate us towards better performance?

In his book *No Contest: The Case Against Competition, Why We Lose in the Race to Win*, psychologist Alfie Kohn reviews the research and concludes that 'superior performance not only does not require competition; it usually seems to require its absence.' In fact, he says, a competitive system perpetuates itself by keeping self-worth low and making even the winners constantly needy of more success. 'We compete to overcome fundamental doubts about our capabilities and finally, to compensate for low self-confidence.'

In other words, when we view life through the lens of competition, we'll always end up feeling small. This point is dramatised in political scientist Xandra Kayden's book *Surviving Power* about ex-politicians and their experience of leaving office. Some 'survived,' while others sank into depression.

The trappings of power can feel great. As deputy mayor, I began to think of myself as a Very Important Person indeed. I thought, I deserve to have 50,000 city employees stand to attention when I enter a room. TV news reporters follow me around because everything I say is meaningful!

But then our term ended. Los Angeles elected a new mayor and, suddenly the camera bulbs stopped flashing in my direction. I was forced to look in the mirror and face up to the question:

If I'm not the deputy mayor of Los Angeles, then who am I? I was adrift. I'd spent so many years chasing after external rewards that my internal self had gone missing.

I was thirty-five, with a lot of living still ahead. It was time to identify and build upon what was unique about me, away from the public eye. It was then, after I left office, that I began to amass the true power that comes from within.

He who dies with the most toys leaves the world empty-handed just like everyone else.

This can be rather confusing. After all, from the moment we start school, we're trained to see all the people around us as names and numbers ranked from high to low. As students, our 'job' is to get to the top. Once we leave school and enter the real world, however, the giant spreadsheet disappears.

When we live our lives through the prism of hyper-competition, we only diminish ourselves. The world always will contain people who are more successful, and those who are less successful than you and I. All of that is completely irrelevant to our lives. Other people are not our standard. Your journey is different from mine, and our journeys are different from those of any other person.

As humans, we are naturally linked, not ranked. So let's revel in the fabric of our shared humanity. Indeed, we all are more alike than we are different. When we understand this, we can much more effectively relate to those around us.

We choose the lenses through which we see reality

People sometimes ask why I'm always so joyful and lively. My reply is that I have very little stress in my life. Then they ask, 'What? Everyone has stress!'

I used to have stress. During my twenties, I was the most hard-working, ambitious, impatient person you ever met. One graduate degree was not enough; I wanted two; at the same time; while I was still working. I was a perfectionist, which is to say that I was stressed out all the time. My 'work hard, play later' attitude meant that happiness was a thing to be deferred, a prize to be grabbed after many more years of hard work, someday, when I retired, perhaps.

I've since come to realise that 100 per cent of the stress in our lives results from our wishing that the entire universe would magically realign itself to conform to our personal agendas.

But that's not how the universe operates. Nobody ever gets that much power. Other human beings are just too elusive. We cannot ever control everyone and everything that happens.

The only person we have any hope of changing is ourself, and if you've ever tried to change yourself, you know how hard that is to do! So imagine how impossible it is to change someone else.

Besides, by now I've lived long enough to see that everything that's ever happened to me that seemed horrible at the time has in the long run turned out to be not so bad after all, or has even resulted in other good things. When I was a child, Chinese and lonely in a white America, I hated being an outsider, but now I see how my outsider's perspective has benefited me profoundly. Every romantic breakup I've had has taught me something about relationships and about myself. Most of the events that caused me tears during my twenties and thirties, I don't even remember now.

My entire life has been a gigantic illustration of a blessing in disguise. Understanding this has allowed me to give up a lot of the confusion, anger and jealousy that used to plague me.

The universe does not conspire to make us happy. Understanding this is sad at one level, but at a deeper level it's liberating. If we're constantly upset by the deviations between how we want other people to act and how they actually do act, then we consign ourselves to lives of anxiety and frustration.

Over the course of my life, I've met and known thousands of people. Each person has taught me something new and has shaped how I look at the world. Together, they taught me that our lives are governed not by facts, but by stories.

A fact is something that can't be refuted and can be objectively verified by anyone. A story is something we create to make sense of the facts around us. How we feel about everything—our salary, our marital status, our life prospects—is based not on universal facts, but on how we look at those things. And from the way we look at the world, we construct the stories that govern our lives.

What makes people complex are the diverse and opposing lenses through which we each view reality. People are irrational, but it's by understanding the ways in which we're all emotional beings that we learn how to deal with them.

When we're children, our lenses are passed down from our parents. The process of growing up is the process of learning how to choose the lenses through which we'll view the world. In fact, as adults, the most important power we possess is the power to select and constantly change the lens through which we see reality.

To me, the metaphor of lens-selection is especially meaningful because all my life until recently, I was so near-sighted as to be classified legally blind. As a child, I saw the world through thick glasses and then, later, through special contact lenses. Each morning when I awoke, I stumbled out of bed and to the bathroom where I inserted my 'eyes'.

Five years ago, I had laser eye surgery which corrected my vision instantly. Now, each morning when I awaken, I roll over, look at the clock and rejoice at the miracle of clear vision.

Age has gifted me with vision correction for life.

Children's fairy tales always end with a happy ending, followed by the words, 'and so they lived happily ever after'. This gives the impression that happiness happens as a result of all the circumstances falling perfectly into place. But life doesn't happen that way, does it?

I love this wonderful couplet from the seventeenth-century English writer John Milton's epic poem *Paradise Lost*:

The mind is its own place, and in itself

Can make a heav'n of hell, a hell of heav'n

Life is utterly unpredictable, but when we take responsibility for owning our own lives we remove the power from other people to make us happy or sad. We stop being victims of the people and events in our life. When things don't go according to our plans, we don't stumble and fall down. Life stops being something that happens to us.

Getting through the rough spots builds resilience. If we know how to make the most of a situation, then we can be powerful and happy even when there are setbacks along the way. When we understand this, we can be joyful regardless of our circumstances, because just as unhappiness is a lens that we construct, we can construct a new lens to bring us calm, joy and success.

How we look at the world is within our power. We can stop being victims of our circumstances, stop grieving when things don't go according to our wishes, and instead focus on how we respond to life as it happens. We owe it to ourselves to actively select and constantly refocus our lenses.

That's when we can create the relationships and the lives that are perfect for us. True power lies not in controlling what happens to us, but in using what happens to us. And within that power lies the beauty of life.

The world loves a happy person

Often, we focus on what we don't have. 'Boy, I'd be happy if only: I get that promotion, I find Mr Right, I get a 7-series BMW.' It's a vicious trap to waste energy wishing for something we don't have while ignoring all that we do have. We need to practice the 'discipline of gratitude'.

Oprah is one of America's richest and most powerful women. She's had a profound effect on American culture and society. She's so famous she doesn't even need a surname. What makes her so powerful? In her words, 'The single greatest thing you can do to change your life today would be to start being grateful for what you have right now. And the more grateful you are, the more you get.'

To be grateful is to be receptive to how much life gives you. It's independent of external circumstances. What if, for example, you have a boss who's an arrogant, morally reprehensible idiot? Even more reason why you must not give him control over your life and happiness.

Gratitude is a way of being, a way of seeing life and of noticing and relating to other people. It's the result of hundreds of decisions each day to choose thankfulness over complaining and bitterness.

Gratitude is a discipline, in the sense that training for an athletic event is a discipline. Like any discipline, it takes practice and can be difficult at times. You can practice the discipline of gratitude in different ways. Oprah keeps a 'gratitude journal' in which she reflects each evening on five things that she's grateful for that day.

You alone are responsible for your own joy. The amazing thing about continuously cultivating the joy that comes from gratitude is that success multiplies in your life. Your joyful attitude causes more good things to happen to you. The world loves a happy person. When we're happy, we smile a lot, and our radiance becomes contagious. Our happiness acts as a magnet, causing other people to want to be with us, to connect with us and to help us.

In fact, happiness has magical properties. Studies show that the happiest people live nine years longer than unhappy people. This is a huge effect, considering cigarette smoking can knock only three years off of your life, six if you really smoke a lot.[1]

All this becomes easier as you get older. Older people are happier than younger ones. In a study of 50,000 Americans, University of North Carolina professor Yang Yang found that being older confers happiness because with age comes positive traits such as self-integration and self-confidence, and these by-products of maturity contribute to a better sense of well-being.[2]

Jolie laide

Los Angeles is a great place to ponder the phenomenon of beauty, our city being known as the world's capital of beautiful people. Each year from throughout rural America, beautiful teenagers flock here in droves to pursue their dreams of becoming movie stars. They're everywhere here, the 'actors/models/whatevers,' sitting in sun-drenched cafes, hoping to be discovered by the next hot Hollywood director.

When my single male friends move to Los Angeles they typically spend the first few months wandering about as if in a fog, eyes popping out of their heads at all the picture-perfect women. They wander around our streets, our grocery stores, our coffee shops, agog.

It takes them a few months to get their bearings. Before even trying to set them up with my single women friends, I wait to let them get their fill of actress-dating. Inevitably, they conclude, 'No more actresses. They're crazy!' I feel for the actresses in our city. When you're in an industry where your entire future depends on conforming to external ideals of beauty, it's hard not to get muddled.

Leave it to the sophisticated French to devise a concept of female beauty so abstract, so nuanced, as to defy logic entirely. Their slangy noun and adjective *jolie laide* literally translates as the contradiction 'pretty-ugly', but think of it as 'oddly beautiful'. Use it this way:

> He scanned the crowd expertly, passing over the typical blondes, and was immediately captivated by the *jolie laide*; with her oversized nose and coquettish eyes, she moved languidly in a vision of urbane elegance.

Jolie laide hints at a world where it might not be just OK, but uniquely beautiful, to be a little odd. It means that a woman can be irregular and yet still wonderful to look at.

I love this concept, *jolie laide*. It's not the uncomplicated, rural-America pretty of *Playboy* bunnies. It's not the perfect-symmetry-pretty suggested by my cosmetic-surgeon friends at dinner parties, 'See that? I can take care of that!' No, as I get older, I find myself increasingly drawn to the more interesting, complex beauty implied by *jolie laide*.

At this point, some of my feminist sisters may sigh that I'm surrendering women being objectified by the male gaze.

But as human beings, we're all drawn to beauty, and I believe that beauty carries its own power. I love *jolie laide* by placing that power within reach of all women.

In fact, I think of *jolie laide* as not passive at all, but a very active form of beauty. This is because it arises not from a surgeon's scalpel or an expensive skin potion, but rather from within the soul of a woman.

Me, I never was a conventional beauty. I have funny dimples on my cheeks. My face, with its swooping angles and planes, is growing more angular with each passing year.

Jolie laide offers hope for the rest of us. It opens up the democratic possibility that a woman can be beautiful because she thinks she is, in spite of her oddities. She loves herself, and that love shines through in how she carries herself, how she expresses herself to the world. Others who would not otherwise be drawn to her looks are yet enchanted because of who she is.

To be a *jolie laide* requires both the *jolie* (pretty) and the *laide* (ugly). The *jolie* stems from what's outside; the *laide* radiates from within.

Who is not *jolie laide*? Maggie Cheung. I love and admire Maggie Cheung. But her beauty, inside and out, is so luminous, so ethereal, so otherworldly, as to be incontrovertibly undemocratic. Maggie Cheung is not *jolie laide* because she lacks a single molecule of the requisite *laide*. For the same reason, I disqualify Fan Bingbing—*pas de laide*.

Who is *jolie laide?* I propose the following women:

- Sarah Jessica Parker. People accuse her of having a face shaped like a horse's, but it's her horse-shaped face, and she does wear it beautifully, along with every other thing she wears. I still miss *Sex and the City*, the TV version, but it's always fun to see her pop up in magazines and fashion venues. SJP is a regular presence in my life, and I like it that way.

- Kristin Scott-Thomas. Another lovely animal-shaped face, this one shaped like a duck's. So acutely talented, so witty, ironic, elegant, an Englishwoman who's lived in France since age nineteen, Kristin to me represents the very best of both the English and the French. *Magnifique*!
- Marion Cotillard. With her sleepy/sultry eyes, Parisian Marion Cotillard's look is not at all cookie-cutter, and thus, I think it would have been hard for her to have made it big first in American Hollywood. Marion so naturally balances art, fashion, film, music and environmental causes in just her own way. And she's *ravissant* in her campaign for Dior.

Shu Qi and Karen Mok. As I'm in Los Angeles, I don't know many Chinese celebrities, but to me these are two *jolie laide* stand-outs. Shu Qi with her wide-set eyes, and Karen Mok with her long face, are so fresh and so gifted as to redefine pretty. I hope they go global across the Pacific, because I want to see more of them both.

Each of these women offers prodigious creative talent coupled with a beauty all her own. Each has not only avoided being submerged by society's norms, but has transcended and redefined those norms, establishing herself as an icon of beauty for our generation.

A *jolie laide* radiates with her own grown-up sophistication, her own delicious sense of innuendo. She's independent. She's an original. It's her very own particular *je ne sais quoi* that the world finds simply irresistible.

'But do men like *jolies laides*?' That's the question I got from a Global Rencai reader to my blog post on this subject.

The world contains common, unexceptional men seeking simple, uncomplicated young girls, but you are not interested in such men, are you? You want an exceptional man who will have a singular love for exceptional you. The way to attract him is to revel in and then radiate outward your own unique beauty.

Chapter 9

Should You Have Sex with Your Boss to Get Ahead?

Wonderful etiquette is about respect for yourself and others. It costs nothing but can help you achieve everything.

—Yue-Sai Kan

Dave is a master poker player, and in poker there's an old saying, 'If you look around the table and you don't know who's the chump, you're the chump.'

It's the same way in office politics. If you hate office politics, that's a signal that you need to master the rules of the game. Do yourself a favour and pick up every one of those novels written about Du Lala.

Du Lala was promoted because she has great empathy. She is highly aware of her own feelings and of other people's feelings. That makes her savvy at negotiating her way through the political minefields prevalent in all companies. In her words:

When your boss asks you something, figure out what he really means. He could be just showing off. Understand this and be aware of his true intent.

Some things you should report to the company, and some you shouldn't. When you do report something, be shrewd enough to find the right person/department/resource to report it to.

Really understand your boss and tell him what he expects and wants to hear. Understand his mindsets and priorities. What he tells you to do, do immediately as told. When problems arise that are meaningless to him, solve them quietly without bothering him. With things he wants control over, don't take any liberties. Just advise and remind him.

Be very savvy and good at execution. If the boss asks you to do something, and you finish it without delay, and deliver a great result, how could he not like you?

Lala understands that her boss is not her parent. She understands that it's not his job to take care of her. He's focused on his career. It's her job to take care of him. For understanding and acting upon that, she'll keep getting promoted.

We all want to be successful. So you may be tempted to ask, 'If part of being successful is learning to take care of my boss, how far should I go in taking care of him? Should I go all the way?

Should you have sex with your boss to get ahead?

I'm reminded of an iconic 1990 American movie, *Pretty Woman,* in which Julia Roberts plays a lovely, good-hearted prostitute here in LA. She gets hired by a rich businessman (Richard Gere) in town for a week-long business trip. They stay in a beautiful suite at the Four Seasons Hotel, he buys her fabulous clothes on Rodeo Drive, and he ends up as her boyfriend, giving her enough money to leave prostitution and go to college.

The movie is one of the important movies of American pop culture and typical of the 'American Dream' that says that anyone can get ahead through cagey hard work and a little luck. Plus a little sex with a boss who can change your life for the better.

Outside of Hollywood, however, sex with your boss is not a viable career strategy. The 'sleep-up strategy,' as one of my blog readers calls it, may sound good in theory, but it's much more likely a career-ender than a career-helper.

Everyone gossips, and the #1 thing that everyone gossips about is who is having sex with whom. Once your co-workers start noticing the sly glances and little pet names that you and your boss share, your image will be formed no longer by your outstanding workplace contributions, but by a reputation as a person so incompetent that you had to resort to sex to get ahead.

Your jealous co-workers will find ways to undermine you that you'll never even know about. Even the promotions that you rightfully earn will be cast as evidence of unfair treatment. This is the sort of reputational damage that can follow you for years, anytime your name comes up, 'Ah yes, Jenny, you know she slept her way up.'

And all that is if your romance goes well. If it ends badly, you may have a hard time getting from him any more of the plum assignments, exposure and supervisorial support that are crucial to career success.

If you and your boss decide you want to pursue a romantic relationship, go together to your company and request that one of you be reassigned. Do this before he gives you any new assignments or other workplace benefits. This is important not only for your career, but also to allow you and him to relate as equals. Bottom line:

- Rule #1: No sex with your boss.
- Rule #2: If you break rule #1, either stop having sex with him, or stop having him as your boss.

Should you make love with your co-workers?

Having a smashing career is a great way to expose yourself to good men. But because you should always be discreet in your dating, it's best to date men whom you meet through work who do not actually work in your office. Men you meet at industry cocktail receptions, for example, or those you meet while travelling on business.

But what if Mr Right is sitting in the next cubicle at work? After all, your co-workers are often the people you spend the most time with, and anytime you get men and women together in close quarters for hours on end, well, you know what happens. Sometimes, 'accidents.' Sometimes, longer-term romances.

If you find yourself having a crush or a romance with someone at your office who is not your boss or your subordinate, remember this rule: Separate your love life from your professional life.

Don't fantasise about him. Don't spy on him. Don't constantly look over and stare at him. Stay busy with your work. Don't look for excuses to go by his desk. If your work requires you to talk with him, then talk with him, but be professional. If he hangs around your desk, give him a few minutes, then stop the conversation, 'We'd better get back to work!' If he QQs you, only occasionally QQ him back, and don't do so right away.

Respect the company's communication protocol. If he has a secretary, go through his secretary to set up work-related meetings and calls. Don't write anything personal in your company emails. Don't leave cute notes where others can see them. Don't even leave cute notes where only he can see them. You can do all of that when you're not on company time.

Do not discuss the relationship with any of your co-workers, and tell him not to talk about it. Don't put any photos or anything else about your relationship on your desk. Do not hug, kiss or hold hands in front of anyone work-related.

All these 'don'ts' are for the health of your career as well as for the health of your relationship. Let your relationship unfold naturally without the pressure of everyone watching.

What if your boss sexually harasses you?

Sometimes, however, the romantic attention is unwelcome. In 2010, when Sunmoon Education Group CEO Song Shanmu was arrested for raping his employees, blog readers asked if I would comment on what you should do when you are sexually harassed.

My first reaction was, 'No, thanks!' That's because sexual harassment is a highly sensitive subject for the CEOs and HR chiefs who hire headhunters like me. It seemed imprudent for me to blog about a subject that would just annoy my clients.

But I did some research, and found that sexual harassment is prevalent in workplaces across Asia. I recalled when I was sexually harassed two decades ago. And I thought, with the profile I've been lucky to build in my career, if I don't stand up and speak publicly about this topic, who will?

Then, I struggled with what to write. Finally, I muddled my way through a blog post, offering what was a decidedly imperfect solution. I posted it late on a holiday weekend, thinking it might slip by unnoticed.

But then, Xu Qinduo, host of *Today on Beyond Beijing* on China Radio International, and Ji Xiaojun, host of *Crossover* on CCTV News, each decided to devote an entire show to sexual harassment and asked if I would be willing to be featured.

I didn't want to be known as the 'sexual harassment lady', but I did feel inspired by the fact that two such respected media leaders wanted to bring this subject out into the open. So I agreed.

Those shows have touched off a stream of notes and messages to me. I've been especially touched by the grateful notes from those viewers who were and are victims of harassment.

On the CRI show, women's rights attorney Zhang Weiwei celebrated the outcome of China's first legal victory for a victim of sexual harassment, in which the woman won a RMB 3,000 judgment against her boss but lost her job. I have mixed feelings about this. On one hand, I believe that we all owe a debt of gratitude to Zhang Weiwei and all women's rights lawyers working tirelessly to lead our society forward.

On the other hand, as a headhunter, I feel that while this case was not a victory for the brave victim who stepped forward. Her compensation was paltry, certainly not enough to justify stalling her career over, and probably not enough to serve as a deterrent to other would-be harassers. I believe the lesson here is that we need to redouble our efforts to rid our society of abuse against women, while at the same time protecting ourselves when it does happen.

I was harassed once, early in my career, by the CEO of the company I worked for at the time. Whenever he saw me alone he would come up from behind me and start kissing and licking my ears and neck. I remember how nervous and powerless I felt whenever I was at work. The only way I knew how to end the harassment was to quickly find a new job and leave the company, which is what I did. I was lucky the harassment never became violent, but decades later, the memory of his actions still makes my skin crawl.

Nowadays, on sexual harassment there's the party line, and then there's the truth. The party line of corporate CEOs and HR chiefs is this: 'If you are harassed, report the incident to the HR department of your company.'

But the truth is that claims of sexual harassment typically lead to retaliation against the victims. And here, the atmosphere at foreign companies is not necessarily better than at Asian ones.

According to one well-known Beijing-based management consultant who works with both Asian and foreign companies:

> If a woman goes to HR with a problem, the company most likely will protect the manager and alienate the victim. Most likely, the woman making the complaint will see her career suffer. Also, once a woman goes public with a case, it is likely that other future employers will not hire her as she might be perceived as a troublemaker.

A sobering assessment. This issue is so sensitive that my friend asked me not to use his name or the name of his firm.

When it comes to sexual harassment the question, sadly, often is not 'if' but 'when'. According to a 2005 survey cited in Chinese state media, only 21 per cent of women say they have never faced sexual harassment.[1] On the other hand, a study by Oxfam India 'Sexual Harassment at Workplace in India 2011-12' found that only 17 per cent of working women had claimed to have experienced sexual harassment.

Guo Jianmei, the founder and president of the Beijing Zhongze Women's Legal Counseling and Service Center, says this:

> Workplace sexual harassment is an increasingly serious issue. China's legal system is not currently set up to deal with sexual harassment. It only states that sexual harassment is prohibited, but doesn't propose any real guidelines on how to prevent or punish it. Women should be cautious and protect themselves. For example, when it happens, a woman should strongly say no, and she should keep evidence in case legal action is needed.

If you are sexually harassed, and there's someone in power in HR whom you feel you can trust, I suggest you confidentially report the harassment to him or her. But more often that will not be the case. So in general, I suggest that you focus on how to stop the harassment without harming your career. I reluctantly endorse the advice of careers blogger Penelope Trunk in her blog post 'Don't Report Sexual Harassment':

- Have a frank conversation with your harasser. Be specific about what behaviour is making you uncomfortable. Tell him that you prefer not to go to HR about it. He won't want that either, because no matter how arrogant he is, he'll not want to get into a messy he-said-she-said situation with you.
- Lay out your negotiating position. Aim high. You want his help to transfer to a better position in the company, with a different boss, or you want his help in finding a better job outside of the company.
- If the balance of power is not in your favour, and you get nowhere negotiating, find a new job and leave the offending company—in that order—because it's always easier to find a job when you have a job.
- Do take the steps needed to protect yourself, which may in the end require leaving the company, reporting the harassment to HR or company management or even to the police.[2]

It is clearly unjust for the onus to fall on you to single-handedly right the wrong that's been done to you. Professionally speaking as a headhunter, I hate to advocate a solution that tolerates abuse and thus, does not contribute to building great or lasting companies. But we do not yet live in a world where we can trust employers to do the right thing when alerted to sexual harassment in their ranks. Or in a world where we can trust the legal system to make whole the many women who get harassed.

And so, it makes me sad to say this, but the truth is that if you are harassed, it's likely that your best course will be to quietly leave your company as I once did many years ago.

The biggest reason that workplace harassment has declined in the US is that when harassment occurs, companies are held liable, and in the past two decades, several high-profile cases involving deep-pocketed employers and huge payouts to victims have led employers in general to implement internal reforms.

I believe there are 'carrot' and 'stick' incentives for companies to prevent harassment in their ranks. The 'stick' of lawsuits is important, but over time, I believe that the companies that win in the marketplace will be those that recruit and retain the best talent. And the best talent does not choose to work in abusive environments.

There is plenty to do in this world that does not require you to work in an environment where you are being harassed. There are plenty of men and women out there who value a work environment in which women are respected. Find those men and women and work with them. Then, accumulate power in your career and create the kind of workplace you believe in. By committing to create strong workplace cultures, we can build and lead the great companies of the future.

Chapter 10

Where are All the Good Men?

Women or men, we all share a core humanity.

—Lifen Wang

During my twenties, I dated around but in general my love life was somewhat unsatisfying. Boys aged eighteen worshipped me; man-boys aged fifty worshipped me more. Guys my own age seemed a little unfinished, like I was.

My girlfriends and I spent many evenings together over cocktails dissecting the men we knew, and wondering, Where are all the good men? Often, we felt like the nutty, lovable Elaine of the TV show *Seinfeld:* 'I'm not a lesbian. I hate men, but I'm not a lesbian.'

The problem with men today

Men have it pretty good, don't they? Cared for by mothers when they're young, cared for by wives when they're grown. Unaccountable for housework and childcare at home, occupying most of the leadership roles at work.

All this power, however, comes from a Faustian bargain. In the classic German legend, Faust is a successful scholar, but he's dissatisfied with his life. So he makes a deal with the devil Mephistopheles. He receives unlimited knowledge and all worldly pleasures in exchange for his soul.

A man's power is built on unstable sand. Society judges him by one measure: Being successful at work in order to provide for his family. His worth is based on the size of his financial assets, a matter over which he does not have full control. A *New Yorker* cartoon shows two well-dressed men at a bar. One says to the other, 'Money is life's report card.' Society objectifies women, but it objectifies men as well.

There's nothing wrong with competing as long as you don't rely on the competition to achieve a sense of worth, and as long as you're not devastated if you don't win. But in our society, if a man has no money, he has no value. Winning equals making the most money. If a man is not a winner, he's a loser. And the cost of losing is more than the game in front of him. It's abandonment.

Movies and video games for boys are packed with messages where being strong means being violent and hurting people. 'Real men' are tough guys like Arnold Schwarzenegger who speak in short sentences like 'I'll be back.'

Being male means being aloof, unfeeling and armed with weapons. Bachelorhood is not only not a cause for worry, but is even sexy. If a man is caught caring for his wife, he puts his manhood at risk, and thus, the endless jokes about sissified husbands who help with the cooking.

To be a man is to be strong and independent, to rule in solitary splendour. Men are taught to avoid being dependent on or even influenced by other people as anyone should be in any relationship. Flooded with all these messages, many men become emotionally detached and have trouble making friends. All this comes at an enormous personal cost to them as well as to those who try to love them.

Human beings can tolerate alienation for only so long. In the words of American philosopher Henry David Thoreau, 'The mass of men lead lives of quiet desperation.' In his bestselling book *I Don't Want to Talk About It: Overcoming the Secret Legacy of Male Depression*, psychologist Terrence Real writes:

> Unlike traditional mythic images of the lone, utterly self-sufficient hero, real boys and men need social connection just as much as do girls and women. A sense of self-worth implies a secure sense of membership, of mattering to someone, of being worthy of intimacy. In a healthy relationship to performance, achievement is a labour of love that exists within the context of secure connection, not an act of grandiosity that takes the place of connection.

And thus, the cruel irony of men's lives today, Society trains men to strive for achievement in order to be worthy of love, and yet their very drive to achieve isolates them from human contact. It's hard being a modern woman but it's hard being a modern man as well.

Lack of love between men and women is nothing new in history. The reason our mothers and grandmothers never expected to have love in their marriages is that love never has been a part of our Asian tradition in which women submit to men.

Hierarchy is antithetical to love, because real love can only exist between two people who are both free. Where one is subject to the other, there can be gratitude and piety, but not love. Throughout Asian history until now, our family structure replaced love with submission.

Given this context, then, we can start to understand the radical nature of love between a man and a woman. Passionate love could only exist on the edges of our old social order. When it existed, it was always violently stamped out. The Butterfly Lovers and Heer–Ranjha died because they had to die.

Yet the legend lives, as clear and lyrical today as ever. Because it speaks to the yearning in all our souls—women's as well as men's—to open up and be seen and loved and touched by another human being, to experience joy and delight and all that makes us human.

The reason it's so hard to find a good man these days is because we're the first generation to demand love, and yet neither we nor men have been taught the skills to achieve that love.

But herein also lies the reason to have hope for today's women to find the good men we want, because men need what we need. It's testament to this need that so many men are stepping forward and reaching out to women with love and partnership in the home.

Is it OK to be with a man who makes less money?

I often receive notes from readers like this one:

> Joy, I've worked hard and I have a great career and make lots of money. I love to travel and hang out with my girlfriends and spend my money. My problem is

that I can't find a man who's more successful than me. They're all married or gay.

This issue goes to the crux of all our cultural notions of what it means to be a man and what it means to be a woman today. After all, forever in Asian history, for a man to be a man, he had to dominate; for a woman to be a woman, she had to submit.

If we want to be equal to men, and if we want to free ourselves from the hierarchy that has always put us in a submissive role, then we need to be willing to discard the notion that men must be dominant. And if we want to transcend society's objectification of women and men, then we need to get beyond the idea that the only way to evaluate a man is through his financial worth.

Yes, it is OK to be with a man who makes less money than you. Warren Buffet, a man who knows a thing or two about money, advises, 'It's better to hang out with people better than you. Pick out associates whose behaviour is better than yours and you'll drift in that direction.'

The reward for moving beyond society's dehumanising views of men and women is the possibility of having a real partnership in which you and he are lifelong lovers and true partners. Domestic partners, who share in the joys and work of family. Career partners, who encourage and share in the battles and triumphs of each other's careers.

Besides, sad as this may seem, given the sexism and other factors that hold women back, there's a very real possibility that a man who makes less money than you now will earn more than you ten years from now.

For some couples, equality means that either the wife

or the husband downshifts a career in order to focus on the family. I've actually seen this work, when I was at Heidrick & Struggles.

Global executive search is a demanding business. It pays well, but it involves a huge amount of travel. At Heidrick, the long-running inside joke had to do with the fact that nearly all the senior-ranking women in the firm who had kids also had stay-at-home husbands, some enjoying their retirement, others just enjoying their golf game.

We called them the 'Heidrick husbands'. It goes without saying that the Heidrick husbands had lots of paid help, since most men with money choose not to handle the housework or childcare on their own. As far as I know, the arrangements were happy ones for all.

Those of us who didn't have kids but wanted them would joke to the CEO, 'Hey, when will you be issuing me my Heidrick husband?'

Learn to be a headhunter

By buying this book, you declared that you're not the type of woman who's content to marry just anyone. Admit it, ladies. If all you wanted was to be married, you'd be married by now, right? To that guy who's always loved you. Who's always around, anytime you need help buying a new computer, studying for a test or fixing the kitchen drain. If you just gave him the chance, he'd marry you. But you don't want him. You are exceptional, and you're looking for your match.

But how do you find him?

If you were in the market for a new car, you wouldn't

run out, buy the first one you see, bring it home and test-drive it for six months or a year before bringing it back and trying another one. So why would you shop this way for a man? Be a headhunter.

For a search to be successful, first you need a clear picture of who you're looking for. Without this picture to guide and discipline your search, you'll search aimlessly, always susceptible to being pulled off course. As a result, you could easily end up stuck for years trying to make a relationship work with Mr Wrong. Worse, you could marry him.

Anytime I meet a new client for my headhunting firm, we first discuss the status of his company and his strategy for the future. We talk through the challenges facing the new CEO, or chief marketing officer, or CFO or whatever search I'm there to discuss. Then, I construct a candidate profile. This profile has three 'buckets':

BUCKET A: Knowledge, Skills and Qualifications. The candidate's past experience and education, knowledge and technical skills. In other words, everything that's on his resume.

BUCKET B: Leadership Competencies. How the candidate actually behaves in the workplace. We identify the most important leadership behaviours that will be needed for success in this particular position.

BUCKET C: Personal Characteristics. Who this candidate is as a person. His values and motivation.

I break out the criteria like this because, in my experience, companies on their own often hire on the basis of bucket A—the resume—and yet promote and fire based on buckets B and C—how this person actually behaves and who this person actually is.

This disconnect between what clients think they need and what they actually need can result in huge costs and missed opportunities, both for their companies and for the individuals they mistakenly hire. That's why it's so important to agree, up front, on what we're looking for in a candidate.

Ask a good man what he's looking for in a woman, and he'll say four things: Pretty, nice, smart, confident. But ask a modern woman what she wants in a man, and she'll rattle off fifty things: Owns a nice apartment, drives a hot car, has a top-calibre graduate degree, has the chequebook of Mukesh Ambani, the looks of Hrithik Roshan, dresses extremely well but not too gay, knows how to order a nice bottle of wine in a restaurant, knows what to do with the wine when it arrives, and forty-two other things.

Most of these are bucket A attributes. Apartment ownership, top-notch schools and knowledge of wine or clothes all have nothing to do with how he behaves as a boyfriend (Bucket B) or who he is as a human being (Bucket C).

Take it from me. I have more dating experience than you do. After all, I got married at the age of thirty-eight, and I did not spend the previous twenty years playing bridge with the ladies. During my twenties, in my own search for Mr Right, I focused too much on bucket A. The tables got turned on me when I was deputy mayor and, too often, when a man asked me out on a date I suspected that his interest had less to do with 'me' than with my position and how I might be able to help him. It didn't feel good. Nobody wants to feel used.

And by the way, given recent declines in India's and China's real estate market, an apartment may not be a wise or secure financial investment these days. Here's how you should look at money: Find a guy who shares your values about money. If you like money, find a guy who will work for it with you.

Whether for your company or your life, buckets B and C are the real predictors of whether your relationship will last. From your checklist of fifty, identify a few 'must have' qualities.

Realistically, your checklist will include some bucket A items. For example, in my case, I've had a lot of life experiences, and I don't think I could realistically be with someone who isn't well-educated and well-travelled. But winnow those down. Then focus your search on a few crucial buckets B and C items. For example:

- We share similar values; he wants what I want in life.
- He's mature and empathetic.
- I trust and admire him.
- Being with him makes my heart sing.

Move all those other of your fifty criteria to a new 'nice to have' column. Items that belong on this lower priority column are things having to do with how he dresses, orders wine, family reputation, etc.

Don't expect Mr Right to be your everything. As we discussed in Chapter 3, we all need different types of friends in our lives. No one person can be all those different types of friends to you, so don't expect that of your Mr Right.

Don't expect Mr Right to be perfect. Nobody's perfect, not even you. And don't expect him to have everything on your 'nice to have' list. He may turn out to be very different from you, but he will be your perfect complement. Prepare for the inevitable disappointments by learning to truly accept him, not as your prince or your Daddy or your saviour, but as a man and as your partner.

I spent a lot of time dating narcissistic bad boys who had all the 'nice to have' items, 'like very glamorous', 'takes me to exotic locales', 'wears designer clothes', but who lacked crucial 'must have' items, like 'trustworthy' and 'he really loves me'.

It may seem fun at first to jet around with your fancy boyfriend, but if you don't fundamentally like him or feel connected to him as a true friend, the glamorous part gets old. Especially after you and your fantastic girlfriends can afford to jet yourselves around to those same exotic locales and have even more fun.

As for me, I used to think it would be great to marry a Chinese guy. While English has long since become my native language, I imagined that when it came to marriage, it would be really nice and comforting, to go back to speaking Chinese at home. And someday my husband and I might even produce little Chinese babies.

Turned out there were few guys in the higher-level American business and political spheres that I ran in, and ultimately I ended up with someone who knows only a few words in Chinese and speaks most of those in fourth-tone.

Our two baby girls are citizens of the world: 50 per cent Chinese, 25 per cent Hungarian and 25 per cent Italian.

Dave is the funniest and most empathetic guy I've ever met. Everyone who meets him has the same reaction, 'Wow, what a great guy!' All this has a positive effect on his work, since people like him, trust him and then want to do business with him. Every time we see friends, I can't wait to hang out with him afterwards, comparing notes on what was said, and what was *really* said.

Dave lights up my life with his sharp wit and buoyant spirit. He's not bad on the eyes, either.

Chapter 11

Married Men and Other Mr Wrongs

I never rely on men, but I need men.

—Hung Huang

In addition to the 'must have' and 'nice to have' columns, also start a 'no way' column, because some men simply are not marriage material. The first category of men to put in your 'no way' column will be married men.

If you're young and single and you have the requisite female body parts, chances are there's a married man hanging around. Married men can be so flattering. They come bearing goodies, jewellery and expensive handbags and sometimes even a furnished apartment. By and large, they're not just looking for sex. They're lonely, they're attentive, they can help you and you can help them back.

But married men also come with drawbacks. They set the schedule of when you can see each other. They have an annoying habit of disappearing to be with their families on Saturday nights when you most want to see them. When you're out with them in a fancy restaurant, and their wife's friend walks in, they dive under the table, and that's humiliating.

Say no to married men

A reader sent me this:

> I am a married man's lover. He's older than me, a mentor-like figure. I've met his family, friends and buddies, so I'm not totally in the closet. He doesn't get along with his wife, and it's not easy to support a family with a kid. He loves me, but I am not sure if he loves me enough. It will break my heart. I love him, but I hate him more, and I don't know when I can come out into the open. I want to forget about him but I can't stop thinking of him. What should I do?

What should you do? You should dump him.

Maybe he'd gotten married and had kids before he really knew what he wanted out of life. By now, after so many years of marriage, he and his spouse have evolved in different directions.

Well that happens to a lot of people, men and women. But rather than address the situation like a responsible adult, he's trying to hide from it, by running around with pretty younger you.

He may say that he loves you and he can't get along with his wife, but I don't think he's saying the same thing to her. He's betraying her, the woman he promised to love. He's not honouring you either, because he can't love you openly.

I once came across a newspaper column of fifty life lessons by a woman who is a single parent and cancer survivor.[1] At the time, I was in politics, a world full of intrigue and ethical gray areas, and I was struck by this lesson, 'If a relationship has to be a secret, you shouldn't be in it.'

That's great advice for your professional life as well as your personal life. Your secret relationship with this married man is hurting you in two ways. First, it's causing you pain, emotionally and spiritually. Second, it's preventing you from having the type of open, honest, nurturing relationship that you deserve. You may feel noble and loving when you listen to him cry about the sad state of his marriage. But that couple's sorrow is theirs, not yours.

Love yourself enough to be in a real relationship.

By the way, divorced men? Perfectly OK. Many previously-married men never even make it back on the market since they already have wife #2 (or #3 or #4) lined up by the time they divorce. If you do find a good divorced man, don't let his being divorced deter you from dating him. When we met, Dave was divorced with no kids. He's a better man and husband for all the experiences he's had.

In addition to married men, say no to abusers and men with mental-health problems. Please refer to Chapter 6 for a discussion of abuse and abusers. Do such men deserve our empathy? Yes. But there's a bright line between having empathy for someone and dating or marrying him.

I once dated a guy who was a good person in many ways, but who also had a serious destructive streak. I started dating him before I fully recognised it, and then I stayed with him for months too long because I dreaded the pain I knew our break-up would cause to him.

I've since realised that being a nice woman doesn't require you to use up your dating life being a nurse to anyone. I've seen too many families ripped apart over abuse and mental-health problems. If any such problem does arise in your family, get the help you need.

Other men to add to your 'no way' list? Men who don't share your values or your vision for the future. If you value your friends, and he has no friends and is disrespectful to yours, say no. If you want marriage but he doesn't believe in long-term commitment, don't waste your time.

Sharing values also means being able to trust. If you don't feel you can trust your man, carefully consider: Is it your own insecurity, or is it his behaviour? If it's him, say no.

There are no good excuses for cheating, by the way. A man does not accidentally have sex with someone. A man who cheats is someone who has issues to work out within himself. Don't let him work out those issues on your time. Only stay with a man you can trust with your life.

And don't stay with a man who uses you for your money. I keep hearing from friends about the growing problem of 'phoenix men' who use wealthy young women for their family connections and money.

We all start out naïve in love. That's why it's so important to educate and protect yourself, by dating a range of men to improve your powers of evaluation, and by introducing your boyfriends to people who love you and to pay attention to their feedback.

Do not settle for Mr Wrong

My friends and I, all have stayed in relationships longer–months, even years–longer than we know is good for us. We try to change him, we try to change ourselves, we struggle to make a fit where there is no real fit, and in the process of trying to make things work, we make everything worse.

We stay because we don't want to hurt his feelings. We stay because we lack the courage to listen to our hearts. We stay because change is scary, the prospect of being alone is scary, and we feel safer in a bad situation than in venturing out into the unknown. We stay because it feels too hard to climb out, and we're tired, and we don't want to start all over again. The dull ache of being in an unsatisfying relationship seems less sharp than the shattering of a relationship.

And so we stay too long, reliving the good times, reminding ourselves that we can't expect to have everything. We rationalise it to our friends, saying, 'This is what it means to be grown up.' We tell ourselves that a bad relationship is better than nothing.

Nothing could be further from the truth. No relationship is far better than a better-than-nothing relationship.

The biggest mistake that women make in relationships is not saying no. This is a deadly mistake, because the biggest obstacle to finding Mr Right is being stuck with Mr Wrong.

Being with Mr Wrong takes you off the market. You and Mr Right will never find each other if night after night, you're curled up in front of the TV with Mr Wrong. Simple inertia can keep you from experiencing real love for months, for years or for a lifetime.

Moreover, more insidiously, being with Mr Wrong is a huge drain on your essence as a human being. If your primary life relationship is with someone who doesn't fully appreciate and love you, if he criticises you or doesn't cooperate with you, then being with him inevitably will chip away at your soul.

Our society conditions us women to expect so little that we're always staying too long in bad relationships. We find a boyfriend—any boyfriend—and we think it's love, when it's really just that longing for attachment. Each day that we stay is new evidence that we lack power and control over our lives. We let our spirits wither away just so we can have a relationship. In this way, we allow our essential selves—our souls—to be submerged forever.

Don't throw yourself away like this. Don't stay with him because you like his parents. Or because the two of you already share an apartment, a checking account and friends. A relationship must be more than a lifestyle.

Don't stay with him because you feel a sense of obligation to him. You have no obligation to date anyone you do not completely love. It's kinder to be honest than to be fake.

Be honest with yourself on how a relationship adds or detracts from your life. Deep inside, you know when a relationship is not right for you. Don't just live to survive. Do not view yourself as someone who should settle.

Any relationship in which you don't feel truly happy and secure and honoured is not a good enough relationship for you. You are worthy of love and you are worthy of great love. Being in a great relationship is far better than being in a better-than-nothing relationship.

Growing up does not equal giving up. Growing up means finding yourself and becoming independent and learning to take care of yourself. Once you've grown up, then you can find a partnership where your spirit can soar. Saying no sets you free.

How to say no to a man

Sometimes when we fall in love, we confuse 'love' with 'forever'. We think that if we love someone, we should want to be together forever. If someone breaks up with us, we assume that he didn't really love us, and feel rejected and betrayed. 'How can you just end this relationship? I thought you loved me! Why aren't you giving us a chance?'

But love is not enough to sustain a relationship. A good marriage requires much more—shared vision, shared values, among other things. When we understand this, we free ourselves to end relationships without feeling guilty or betrayed. We can say, 'We loved each other, but we weren't right as life partners. Now we each can move on. I feel sad, but I wish you well.'

Hard as it is for us women to say no in our daily lives, the hardest no is the one we sometimes need to say to the man in our lives. And so we lose track of no as an option. This is the reason for many of the troubled relationships in the world.

Headhunting taught me to say no, since rejecting candidates is a routine part of headhunting. On a given search, my team and I typically evaluate hundreds of candidates. As a matter of professional courtesy, we personally say no to all unsuccessful candidates, to advise them of the outcome of the search and to wish them the best. To candidates with whom we had only minimal phone or email contact, we send an email. Candidates with whom we've had more extensive contact, we call. That's given me a lot of practice in saying no.

Saying no to a boyfriend can be really hard. It requires trusting yourself, trusting your own wisdom and trusting in a better future. The only way to overcome the difficulty of saying no is to just do it.

Don't waste your time or his. The best time to say no is as soon as you realise that someone is not going to meet your needs, even if he's a great guy, and even if you've shared some great moments together. That realisation may occur on your first date, in six months or years later.

Here's how: Be clear and simple. Mention the things you like about him. Do not blame him. There is no need to review past events, analyse the relationship or give critical feedback. If you want to dissect all that, call a girlfriend.

If he's sad, be understanding, 'I'm really sorry this is painful for you.' But know that you are not responsible for explaining things to his satisfaction, and it's not your job to fix his pain. If he blames you, don't accept the blame.

After you break up, don't look back. Don't feel like a failure, or feel like you've wasted two years of your life. A relationship is not a failure if you learn something from it.

When you say no to Mr Wrong, good things will happen. You'll gain the self-confidence that comes from truly taking care of yourself, and that comes from the knowledge that you're not a slave to whatever people or events happen to come your way. You're taking your life into your own hands and making things happen in your life.

Learning to say no to a man is crucial to your success as

a woman, because having designed your career and your life so beautifully up until now, the last thing you want to do is to wreck everything by being bound for life to a man who's not right for you. Each time you say no, you'll be closer to saying yes when Mr Right does come along.

You cannot change a man

Has this ever happened to you? You meet a guy, and you decide he's perfect for you. Well, almost. You've identified a few areas for improvement, and after those are fixed, he will be perfect for you.

My women friends and I have invested months and years into dead-end relationships, so I will save all of you a lot of time and grief by telling you right now that: You cannot change a man.

This can be hard for a woman to hear. We're women, which is to say that helping our man to improve makes us feel warm and cozy inside. We're always trying to change our man! That's our job! If we don't tell him, who will?

We see our attempts at male-improvement as loving, but often they make men feel controlled, manipulated and rejected. Your man probably likes his life or else he would change it himself. We can only change our own selves and, as you know, that's hard enough to do.

What you should do is to evaluate whether he's husband material for you. What are the flaws you've identified? Are they little things or big things? Do not try to force a man onto your 'must have' column or off of your 'no way' column. Accept him as he is or find someone else. If you do accept him, learn to accept what he can give you, and forgive what he can't.

'He's just not that into you'

There's a great episode from *Sex and the City* where Miranda has a crush on a guy, but he never asks her out. She dissects the situation with her girlfriends, who spring to her defence, 'But you're beautiful! What guy wouldn't want you?!' They come up with every possible excuse for why he hasn't asked her out.

Then, suddenly, a guy comes along, hears the conversation and shrugs, 'He's just not that into you.'

Those oddly empowering six little words spawned an entire self-help book of that title by the writers of *Sex and the City*. Then that book turned into a movie, of the same title. Here's a synopsis of the book and movie: Men go for what they want. If a man doesn't come running after you, there's one simple explanation. He's just not that into you. That does not detract from how beautiful and amazing you are.

A few illustrations:

- Say he promises to call you, but he forgets. Well, he has a job, right? That means he's not an idiot. He can make phone calls. He went on a business trip? Did he take his cell phone? He didn't forget to call you. He's just not that into you, and he doesn't want you to cry.
- Say he hasn't been able to see you because he's been busy. A man is never too busy to get what he wants. 'Busy' is just guy code for 'He's just not that into you.'
- Say you have a crush on a guy, and you engineer some time for you and him to be alone, on a hike,

say, or another fun activity. And he doesn't make the next move. Why? He's just not that into you.

- Say he says he likes you, a lot, but he's not ready for a commitment in his life right now. Well, you can be sure of one thing, and that is that in five years' time he will be married. To someone else. He's just not that into you.

You get the idea. Those six little words free you to forget about him and move on. Someday, when you do find Mr Right, you won't spend any more time pining for Mr Wrong.

Chapter 12

Even a Successful Woman Can Be a Fox

Security depends on how much your man loves you, but how much your man loves you depends on how much you love yourself.

—Rene Liu

It was Maureen's seventieth birthday dinner. Her closest friends were gathered around a table for ten. The room was draped in shimmery fabric. Maureen herself looked like an angel. Lit by candles, her flowing blonde hair formed a halo around her head. And doesn't everyone look beautiful by candlelight? It felt like a scene from heaven. We called for a speech.

> 'Well!' She began. 'After all these years, the only thing that surprises me....'

This is a woman who knows how to create drama. Everyone leaned forward to catch a pearl of wisdom.

'...is that I am *still* such a fox!'

Maureen *was* still such a fox. And she still is today, years later. Maureen is one of those women who fascinate men. Though she's thirty years my senior, she's always had more men around her on a slow day than I've had on my best. Maureen is at an age where there truly are few available men, and yet they all flock around her.

There are enough good men in the world for you

Most of us lack Maureen's effervescent charisma. And so, we're faced with that most modern of questions facing the modern woman: Will I ever find Mr Right?

Two women have two different attitudes towards men:

> Woman #1: Good men my age are either married or gay. The only single ones left are overgrown boys who only go for younger women because they like their women 'gentle', which is just a code for 'submissive'. I am intelligent, so men are intimidated by me. I will never get a man. I'll just stay home and enjoy an indoors life.

> Woman #2: I am confident that soon I will be married to Mr Right. He will care for me always. Our souls will be connected and so we'll overcome every challenge. Our life together will be beautiful and perfect. I need to be patient and wait for him to appear.

One woman is pessimistic. The other is optimistic. Which woman will get her Mr Right?

Neither.

But why? Isn't optimism a good thing?

Recent science shows that there's just one problem with believing that good things happen to optimistic people, and that is that this belief is completely, 100 per cent, false. In fact, studies show, this type of thinking is dangerous because it actually leads to failure.

Psychologist Heidi Grant Halvorson in her book *Succeed: How We Can Reach Our Goal*s, says that, to be successful, you need to differentiate between 'realistic optimism' and 'unrealistic optimism'.

> Realistic optimists believe they'll succeed, but also that they have to make success happen by choosing the right strategies, overcoming obstacles and working hard. Because they believe the path will be hard, they take action.
>
> Unrealistic optimists believe that success will happen to them, that the universe will simply reward them for their positive thinking. If you raise concerns, they'll accuse you of being negative. Because they focus only on what they want, their naïveté prevents them from achieving their goals.

The more important it is to you that your dream come true, the more idealising will sap your motivation. These results hold true across studies of students looking for jobs after college, singles looking for love and seniors recovering from surgery. Realistic optimists send out more job applications, approach more romantic partners and work harder on physical therapy—in each case, leading to much higher rates of success.

Says Dr Halvorson, 'Whether it's starting a relationship with your secret crush, landing a job, recovering from major surgery or losing weight, research shows that if you don't keep it real, you're going to be really screwed.'

The same effect holds true in pessimism. People who are depressed or have low self-confidence are more likely to think about obstacles, and only about obstacles. 'I am a loser and can't do this' is a bad and self-defeating thought. But 'this won't be easy, and I'm going to have to work hard' is a very good negative thought that actually predicts success.

Don't visualise success. Visualise the steps you'll take in order to make success happen.

Will you succeed in finding your Mr Right? I don't know. What I do know is that if you don't believe you will, you most certainly will not. With men as with much of life, I believe the English playwright William Somerset Maugham said it best, 'It's a funny thing about life. If you accept nothing but the best, you very often get it.'

Recently, I was chatting about love with a romantic young woman. I asked her what she was looking for in a husband. She replied, 'I want a guy who will understand me without my ever having to say anything! I want a man who will just guess my feelings.' She added that most of her friends want the same thing.

'My dear,' I said, 'If you wait for a man to come along who will know your thoughts without your having to tell him, you'll be waiting your entire life.'

Mental telepathy is sci-fi fantasy. It's self-defeating to wish for a man who can somehow read our minds and know instinctively how to love us the way we want to be loved. The reality is that the better we understand ourselves and others, the better we can give and get the love we need.

Don't force every man onto the marriage track

I had a friend, Willie Campbell, who was Maureen's mentor, which I suppose made Willie my great-mentor. She died about ten years ago at the age of ninety-two. Six months after she died, her husband of over sixty-five years, Jack, died. I really miss them both.

One day when I was perhaps twenty-four, Willie saw me moping around, having just broken up with the latest boyfriend *du jour*.

Willie: What's wrong?

Me: I'm sad. My boyfriend and I broke up. He was a nice guy.

Willie: Just because he was a nice guy doesn't mean he was the right guy for you.

Me: But I liked him.

Willie: Joy, young women today need to learn how to be friends with men without trying to force each one onto the marriage path.

Me: What if they're our boyfriends and we're having sex with them?

Willie: So what! Men think differently from us. They add fun and new perspectives to our lives. Young women of your age need to learn to be friends with them. More than one of them at a time.

Willie's so right. Men are different from us and can add so much to our lives. Let's learn to be friends with them.

While you're in headhunting mode, stay busy with your

own fantastic life. When you're passionate about chasing your own dreams you lift the pressure and cause men to run towards you. Let them figure out how to get into your fantastic world.

Some relationships start off with major fireworks. You meet someone, lightning zaps and instantly you're in love. You can't stop staring at each other, you can't be without each other, you can't stop gushing about him to your girlfriends.

But those early fireworks won't last if the two of you don't also simply become friends as well. Put aside your romantic visions about dating and falling in love. If you don't sincerely like him and he doesn't sincerely like you, he'll never be Mr Right.

So be his friend. Smile a lot. Be fun. Be funny. Plan fun things together that you both enjoy, like cooking or hiking or badminton. Thinking of him as a great new friend also will keep you from obsessing over him. After all, when you meet a new woman friend you don't require that she only be friends with you. You do not try to track her movements.

Maintain that same sense of calm about him. He's your friend and you don't get to spy on him when he speaks with other women. By the same token, he doesn't get to spy on you when you see other men (And you are maintaining friendships with other men, right?).

Also behave in other ways as you would with someone whose friendship you value. When you're together, give him your full attention. Encourage him in his work. Notice what's wonderful about him. Be a source of new ideas. Inspire him.

Be happy and a little mysterious

When you're around a man you like, let your inner happiness radiate. If you need a refresher in how to be happy, please review Chapters 3-8. You are happy because you are exploring, you are true to yourself and you're busy making good things happen in your life.

You may not be happy with every aspect of your life, but in your first few dates there is no need to unload on him your complaints about the injustices of life or your baggage from previous relationships. First dates should be fun and light.

A man will feel pressured if you focus too much on him, so don't wait by your phone. Go out, have a life and call back when it fits your schedule. When he does call, don't ditch plans with your girlfriends because you already have a life. Your life. Don't dump it anytime you have a new man. Good men won't appreciate it, and bad men will just manipulate you into giving up too much.

When you're with him, be friendly and flirty, but when you're not with him, be away. Don't text him all the time, and don't let your calls drag on. There is no need to explain where you are at all times. Maintain a little mystery. Your message should be: 'I like you but I don't know if you're the right guy for me. Let's have fun and learn more about each other.'

Don't argue with him over how he chooses to spend his time. If you're annoyed that he's sitting down for yet another evening of sports-watching on TV, don't sit by his side and seethe. Find your own things to do. Put on your make-up and a sexy dress, and go out and have fun with your friends looking gorgeous.

Zeng Zihang, the hot male authority on female charm, writes in his book *Honest, Enjoy and No, Make a Woman Secure*, 'Women's power and charm doesn't come from beauty, but mystery. Remember, men are curious kids and are interested in riddles. Be more mysterious, more charming. A woman in a translucent gown is way more charming than a naked one.'

Say you like a guy, but he doesn't ask you out. What do you do? Sit around longing for him, hoping he'll notice? Stalk him online? Suddenly start texting him all the time? No. You ask him out. Not for dinner in a romantic restaurant, but for a daytime date. Like this:

'My computer died! Can you help me buy a new one?'

'Wanna play badminton? Bet I can beat you!'

'I'm getting a study group together for tomorrow's test. Can you come?'

Then, if he likes you, let him chase you back. If he doesn't like you, move on.

Even a successful woman can seduce

When you're a woman, having a successful career is both good and bad for your love life. It's good because good men like independent women, and women like us know how to be independent. But it can be bad because the behaviours we develop for a successful career are often the wrong behaviours for success in the love department.

As women who achieve, we're used to proving ourselves constantly. No matter how successful we become, people see us first as women, and so it becomes second nature to demonstrate to everyone exactly how impressive we are. Those of us women who climbed our way up the corporate ladder did so by climbing over the men and besting them at their own aggressive male behaviour.

But when a man likes you he's not looking for a partner in business—he's looking for a partner in life. If you confuse this and behave on a date the way you act in everyday life—impressive—you may impress him with your intelligence and capability, and he may want to hire you or do business with you, but that doesn't mean he'll want to date you.

So when you're on a date, don't be the 'boss lady'. Don't talk business, and don't try to attract him with your business acumen. Don't display your debating powers; don't try to trump his comments. You might see yourself as capable, modern, persuasive and confident, having a fun intellectual exchange. But to him you may be coming across as competitive and argumentative. He's not looking for a lawyer; he's looking for a girlfriend.

All this took me many years and a lot of wasted dates to figure out because I am the 'boss lady'! For years, that was me, treating first dates like business dinners, showing off my independence, demonstrating that I am just fine without a man. But just because you don't need a man does not mean that that's the right attitude to lead with on a date. The bigger your job, the harder it is—and more impressive it is to him—to not talk about work, and just be a woman and a human being.

What should you talk about? Personal things. Your family. Movies you've seen. Where you've travelled.

What you like to do for fun. Something other than work, anything other than work. Rather than go into performing mode, reach out and ask about him.

Right about now, some of you may be getting irritated. You might be saying, 'But Joy, this is just how I am! My work is who I am! I love competition! I love talking shop. Are you trying to push us women back to the Dark Ages?'

I know how you feel. We behave in ways for which we're rewarded. In the workplace, we're rewarded for being capable and, that's right, for being 'male'. Is it unfair for the world to demand that after work we switch sides and become 'female'?

Depends on how you look at it. It's not unfair, if being 'female' is being nice and gracious and reaching out to really connect with another human being. That's just good behaviour for any relationship.

A good man may not want someone simple, dumb and uncomplicated, but that doesn't mean he's looking for a work colleague in his home. He's not taking his female work colleague off on a glamorous vacation or making passionate love to her. He's debating company strategy with her. He does respect her, but he doesn't want to come home to her after a long day of work.

He's looking for the woman of his dreams, the woman whom he'll love and be successful for.

So don't try to persuade him that you are deserving. You are deserving! You're a queen! He wants to deserve you! One reason that love is hardest for successful women is that we need to learn to stop impressing, and start receiving the love of a good man.

Anytime you worry too much about someone else's approval, that person will lose respect for you. Let him earn your love.

You're a successful woman, which means that you are highly capable of modifying your behaviour for success. Just as you've learned how to modify your behaviour to make it in a man's world at work, now modify your behaviour to relate to those same men after work.

Let there be a '9:00 am you', and a '9:00 pm you'.

Think of how you are now with your niece or nephew, or how you'll be someday with your own kids. You don't give them a speech in your rockin' high heels and Prada suit. No, you kick off your heels and you smother them with love. You reveal different sides of yourself with different people. When you're with him, let your gorgeous self shine.

Don't get mad at the unfairness of it all. There are worse things in life. If you let him treat you like the queen that you are, then you'll never feel like you need to choose between a great career and a great man. You'll be able to enjoy both. Besides, after working so hard at the office, just sitting back and being beautiful and letting a good man take care of you can be really nice.

In my thirties, as body parts sagged and my spirit soared with a growing confidence in life, something funny happened in my love life. I realised that all along, I'd been developing the emotional skills I needed to find and keep a good man.

That's when, like Maureen, I started attracting a narrower band of men, of much higher calibre. The man-boys disappeared and I was left with powerful, self-assured men. Men who wanted a woman who could challenge them. Dating became fun.

Married friends invited me over for dinner just to hear about my latest dating adventures. My first date with beloved Dave occurred on a Sunday night. On the preceding Saturday night, I had another first date with another highly eligible Dave. My friends thought I was the 'bee's knees' for having a 'Saturday Dave' and a 'Sunday Dave' both lined up in a single weekend.

Monday morning, when they called for the after-action report, I informed them that going forward there would be only one Dave. My secretary, for years having juggled my busy work and social schedule, was surprised to hear that maybe, just maybe, I'd even met my 'every day Dave'.

A headhunter is sexy and strong, and that makes her dangerous. She believes in love, but she loves herself first. If a relationship doesn't work out, she doesn't fall apart. She expects to be respected. She doesn't obsess over anyone's opinion, whether that person is a man or anyone else in her life. She stays centred. She's a catch. All of this makes her immensely seductive. Candidates meet her and exclaim, 'Absolutely! I would love to spend my days with someone like that!'

And she's deadly efficient. When she recognises the right candidate, she pounces. You know you deserve the man of your dreams. It's time to let loose the restless headhunter within.

Chapter 13

Date 100 Men. Three at a Time.

I chose him from a million not out of impulse but because I was sure that he was my Mr Right in terms of character and wisdom. He is my one for a lifetime.

—Hong Ying

Does this sound familiar?

You're a good woman. Smart. On the fast track to success. Respected by your peers. But then you meet a man, and suddenly you can't think straight. You feel all mixed-up inside. You start to exhibit strange behaviour:

- Checking your phone every five minutes to see if he's texted.
- Ditching plans with your girlfriends anytime he asks you out.
- Calling him all the time.
- Spying on his QQ; bribing his friends to spy on him.

- Dissecting his every word with your girlfriends.
- Interrogating him over evidence of any communication with other females.
- Needing to be with him; feeling empty when you're not with him.

You've fallen victim to a strange but common obsessive-compulsive disorder. It's called 'new boyfriend syndrome'. The result? He dumps you.

Why? Because you changed. He liked you for you, before you turned into this faint ghost of yourself. When you rush in like this to tie a man down it's as if you're shouting, 'Pick me! Please!!' Your actions proclaim that you're in love with love, not with him.

Society teaches us to throw ourselves at every man who crosses our path. But if you act that way with a man, he'll feel you're desperate and he's ordinary because you'd act the same way with any man. A man wants you to be with him because you choose to be, not because you need to be. And you should choose to be with him for him.

If you suffer from any form of 'man-obsession' (obsessing over one man), or 'man-addiction' (needing to have a boyfriend at all times), take it as a sign that you need practice headhunting.

Headhunting takes years of practice

Some women date around like boomerangs, in each new guy searching for someone who overcompensates in the one area they found lacking in the immediately preceding boyfriend. Others fall in love practically at first sight, then are shocked when they discover their lover has problems just like everyone else. Others still make the mistake of accepting just any guy, and then spending a lifetime picking at him. Classic newbie headhunting mistakes.

We have a saying in the headhunting business: Headhunting would be simple, if only there were no human beings involved. Indeed, people are complicated, irrational and emotional. That's what makes headhunting, and life in general, fun and fascinating.

That also means that to be an effective headhunter you need a keen understanding of what makes people tick, and that requires lots of experience with people.

That's why our industry is referred to as 'an old people's profession'. It's rare to find a successful headhunter who's younger than early or mid-thirties; most successful headhunters are in their forties through sixties. It takes wisdom, maturity and judgment to guide a search towards the best outcome.

Effective headhunting also requires years of training in the specific skills of our profession. Through focused training and interactions with thousands of candidates we hone our skills of evaluation and seduction. In my firm as in most top-level firms, headhunters are required to apprentice full-time for at least three years before they're considered to lead a search.

You have the disadvantage of not being able to devote yourself full-time to becoming a headhunter. You have a day job, which means that you can't be man-hunting for fifty or sixty hours a week. Also, unlike us, you don't get an endless pool of candidates.

I think you can see where I'm going with this. In your man-hunting, get the practice you need.

Phase One: Date, *at least,* 100 men

A friend once told me she was sad because she'd gone on dates with three different guys and none of those dates had turned into a relationship. As a result, she planned to give up dating for a while. I replied that if she were a headhunter at my firm and she abandoned a search after speaking with just three candidates, she'd be out of a job.

For any given search, the successful headhunter considers an appropriately large field of candidates. My firm routinely reviews hundreds of candidates for every search. Once on a particularly difficult search for a CFO for a Fortune 500 company, we evaluated over 1,000!

You now are a headhunter for the most important search of your life. During the candidate evaluation phase of a search, you must keep your options open. Options are candidates.

Your candidates are men. Maintain a universe of the largest possible number of candidates and carefully evaluate each one. Date, at least, 100 men before choosing your one.

Don't marry your first boyfriend. How could you know it's love if you have nothing to compare it to? Aren't you curious about men? It would be a shame to narrow down all of your life's options because of someone you happened to meet in your youth.

Your single years are your time to find Mr Right and to find yourself. Any time you settle down with any one guy, your life possibilities shrink dramatically. Give yourself time to enjoy your freedom before choosing the man who's right for you.

So don't waste your single years locked away in relationships. This is the only time in your entire life that you'll get a chance to meet, flirt with and date a wide range of men. Falling in and out of love is an important part of your growth and experience as a modern woman.

Single men are everywhere, travelling on airplanes, at hotels, at business conferences, etc. For me, as a real estate developer, as a politician and then as a headhunter, I met thousands of men every year. Additionally, I've been involved in charities and other groups that brought me in contact with more men.

In headhunting, time is money. My firm gets paid over US $100,000 for each search, and for that kind of money, our clients want results, fast. When one of my headhunters is sitting by the phone with a stack of fifty resumes, she spends no more than twenty to thirty minutes speaking with any one candidate. Within that time, she evaluates him against our candidate profile and decides whether to invite him to interview with us in person. Time wasted with any one candidate is time we'll never get back. She moves swiftly and efficiently.

In the case of your search, time is even more precious. Our phone screening phase is like your dating around phase. Use your dating around phase to screen out the vast majority of candidates based on the 'must have' and 'no way' columns from your candidate profile that we developed in Chapters 10 and 11.

When you interview a candidate your job is to simultaneously do two things: Seduce and evaluate. Inexperienced interviewers often get so caught up in the momentum of an interview that they forget to do either.

Look beyond the grand gestures—the expensive restaurant, the huge bouquet of flowers. The little things are more revealing, since in any relationship, character issues are the most important. How does he treat you? How does he treat every single person in his life? How does he rate against the criteria on your 'must have' list? Do you share similar values? Could you see him as your very best friend? What motivates him? How does he behave in different situations? Observe everything.

Be vigilant for any disturbing behaviour. Does he have any of the deadly flaws that show up on your 'no way' list? Does he have a dark side? Does he have any problems with anger management?

Work hard to manage your emotions and maintain your headhunter's objectivity. That means dating should be less a gigantic soap opera and more a process of elimination. It's good seduction strategy to maintain a bit of mystery with any man, but keeping some emotional distance is even more important to your headhunting approach because you need to consider any one man against the entire candidate universe.

You won't have chemistry with everyone, so avoid evaluating each date as a success or failure. Instead, at the end of each date, think about what you learned, and be thankful for that. With each candidate, you're learning to correct yourself and get closer to the target with your next candidate.

When you meet someone special you may feel yourself starting to fall for him. Avoid the temptation to abandon your friends and family. Rather, expose him to them and listen closely to their feedback. At the same time, get to know his friends and watch his behaviour with them. Continue to get to know him and others. Give yourself time between dates to let your life unfold and just think things over. Let him take the lead, give him space. You work hard at your job, so with him relax and have fun.

Even as you evaluate each candidate, keep a pool of other interested candidates nearby and ready for evaluation. Have a smashing career, go to lots of parties, maintain diverse interests and generally, live a fantastic life surrounded by men. All this is important for your own life as a woman of the world, but doing all this is specifically important for your manhunt.

How long should you maintain your candidate pool? Until you have a boyfriend? No. Until you're married.

Meet men through your friends and especially through your acquaintances. After all, if you're single, you may already know all the single friends of your close friends. It's your acquaintances' single friends you don't know.

Challenge men by being sought after. Let multiple men chase you, at the same time. Date them three at a time. Why three at a time? To keep them on their toes and to give you some reference points for comparison. You'll be less likely to try to make someone else your everything.

During the dating around phase, keep things light and playful. Plan most of your dates as fun daytime dates. After a few hours, end the date. Don't have sex (More on that later). If it's evening, look at your watch and say, 'I've had such a nice time! I've got a big day tomorrow, better get my beauty sleep!' Give him a hug or a kiss.

Remember, the world contains many men, and whom you spend time with is completely under your control. Anytime you don't feel a man is right for you, politely say no.

Phase Two: When it's time to date just one

After a few months of dating a man and comparing him to others, you may feel ready to have an exclusive boyfriend-girlfriend relationship with him. Do not forget that during this phase, you're still interviewing him.

Keep your eyes open, watching and evaluating whether he can make you happy in the long run. This is also the easiest time to end the relationship if you don't feel comfortable going to the next step. Spend at least six months together as boyfriend–girlfriend before thinking about marriage.

Men and women have different reactions to sex. A man easily distinguishes between sex and love, thus the existence of prostitution and hard-core porn. But for a woman, sex and love often are inextricably bound. If sex happens too early in a relationship, love often follows, and blindly.

When a man has sex, he thinks, 'That was fun! I'd like to get together with her again!' When a woman has sex, she thinks, 'That was profound! I think I've found my soulmate!' Continuing to have sex with the wrong guy can keep you emotionally locked into a relationship for months and years too long.

So my advice is: Do not have sex before you're officially 'boyfriend–girlfriend', in an exclusive, committed, monogamous relationship. Have a speech ready, 'I just love being with you! But I'm kind of old-fashioned. I only want to have sex with you when we've decided we want to be in an exclusive, committed relationship, and I don't feel we're quite there yet.'

Don't jump into bed. And don't ever use sex to try

to get a man to love you. The purpose is not just to look classy. You need to date around, without sex, to observe and evaluate him. If he really likes you and wants you to be his girlfriend, he'll be happy just to be in your company.

Sex with a new boyfriend often makes a woman feel vulnerable. During and after sex don't initiate a major discussion about your feelings. Don't talk about what this means. Don't ask, 'Now that we've had sex, where is this going?' Start off the next day by letting him suggest a place for breakfast as if it is just another wonderful new day. And ladies, make him use a condom. Every time. A modern woman takes care of herself.

Some women (mostly older ones) are more self-assured and are able to see sex for what it is—a very fun physical act that has only as much meaning as two people imbue it with. Some women just want to have a 'friends with benefits' arrangement with a good friend. If that's you, I don't see a problem with you having your fun. But keep it quiet, and make sure he does, too.

Under no circumstances should you ever feel pressured for sex. Not if you're on your third date with someone, or your three hundredth date with him. Not if he whisks you away for a romantic weekend and is paying for the hotel. Not if he's your boss (Especially if he's your boss). Not even if he's your husband.

No means no, and if he truly respects you, he will respect your boundaries and work hard to create the conditions that will make you feel safe and joyfully in the mood. Don't stay with a man who gives you unwanted pressure to have sex. Find someone who will love you the way you deserve to be loved.

Doubt means no

A blog reader recently asked, 'The biggest problem facing many women is not how to find Mr Right, but that after several years of dating, he still doesn't propose. How do you get a man to commit?'

Men instinctively know that they're headhunters. They are naturally afraid of being trapped with the wrong partner. But since we women bear most of the risks of marriage and parenthood, we should be at least as cautious.

Therefore, do not ever put a man in charge of your relationship. Do not repeatedly initiate 'The Talk'. The Talk is any conversation related to the status of your relationship. Don't ask 'Why haven't you called?' or 'When will I see you again?' Tell him how much you enjoyed being with him, then turn around and walk out of the door. Don't ask, 'Where do I stand?' or 'Where is this going?' or ask to meet his kids. Don't sigh, beg or plead with him to move forward more quickly. Don't overanalyse your relationship.

After a time of exclusively dating without a marriage proposal, some women will start to plot 'The Ultimatum'. It goes like this: 'Hi honey. Propose to me within x amount of time (such as three months), or I will leave you!'

Other women choose to take matters into their own hands by secretly 'forgetting' to take their birth-control pills in order to intentionally-accidentally get pregnant and force a shotgun wedding.

Do not resort to The Ultimatum and absolutely under no circumstances should you ever secretly get pregnant. It is immoral and unfair to trick a man into life's biggest commitment. He may love the baby but he will resent you forever.

Don't spend time with any man who keeps you wondering. Say you've been dating a guy for a while, and you think things are going great, but there's been zero discussion about a deeper commitment, whether it's exclusively dating or marriage. Is he completely clueless? Waiting for someone better to come along? Not a good sign.

Initiate The Talk. Once. Like this: 'Hi honey. I have loved our time together, but I'm starting to sense that you and I might want different things. I'm looking for a longer-term commitment such as marriage and perhaps, children. Are you interested in that? Because if not, I think it might be better for us to part ways so that we each can go out and find what we need.'

Perhaps this talk will prompt him to wake up and realise that he loves you and can't live without you. But if you've let him know you're ready to discuss marriage and he isn't, initiate a separation. If he doesn't come running after you with a proposal, then you'll have stopped wasting your time. Know your own limits and leave when it's time to leave.

If you ever find yourself in a situation where you are considering deploying The Ultimatum or an intentional-accidental pregnancy, take it as a sign that in fact, he is not Mr Right. Marriage must be an active choice for both the woman and the man. We need to move beyond the idea that a man becomes Mr Right simply by virtue of our dating him for a year or more. We need to move beyond the idea that it is a woman's job to entrap a man. The only way that we as women can be free to make our own choices is to encourage men to be free as well. When you're with your soulmate, it should be completely obvious to you both.

Oprah says it best, 'Doubt means no.' If either he or you has any doubts at all about your relationship, do not proceed with life's ultimate commitment. Your goal must be not just to start a marriage, but to do your best to ensure that when you do marry, your marriage is one that thrives. When I look around at my friends who have either divorced or are suffering through troubled marriages, in too many cases they recall sadly how even before their wedding day they had doubts, but did not act upon those doubts.

Do not settle for Mr Wrong. You are worthy of being deeply loved. Your future children deserve to grow up in a home built on mature love, happiness, security and stability.

When a man truly commits himself, you'll know. You'll never have to wonder where he is or whom he's talking with. He'll call you every day; he'll constantly try to please you, because he wants you all to himself, all the time. He'll want to meet your friends. He'll want you to meet his family. He'll open up and share his entire life with you.

He'll be grateful for every day he has with you. Wild horses would not keep him from running after you and making absolutely certain that you are his forever. And he will commit to spending the rest of his days caring for you and any children that you have together someday.

Chapter 14

Make Your Own Life Decisions

Never let other people drive your car of life. Sit in the driver seat, decide when to stop, back up, make turns, speed up and slow down. Listen to other people, but never let them determine your journey.

—Kaifu Lee

Many young couples in love who plunge into marriage do so for the wrong reason. They see marriage like a natural next step, their first step into official adulthood. They're excited about their relationship and just want to get to the next stage in life.

Youth is the #1 obstacle to a good marriage

If during your twenties you sometimes feel that you're only halfway grown up, that's because your brain is only halfway grown up. Neuroscientists once thought the brain stops growing shortly after puberty, but now they know it keeps maturing well into the twenties and the thirties.

This new understanding comes from a longitudinal study of brain development sponsored by the US National Institute of Mental Health, which tracked nearly 5,000 children from childhood through adulthood. The scientists found that the children's brains were not fully mature until at least twenty-five. This discovery was shocking even to the director of the study.[1]

In fact, the part of your brain that keeps changing is the part that comes up with long-range strategy and that answers the question, 'Who am I and what do I want to do with my life?'

That means that you're a different person now in your twenties than you will be in your thirties—and so is your boyfriend. It's natural that a boyfriend you met when you both were twenty-four later grows in a different direction than you. If this happens to you, cut back on your time with him and meet some new friends. As you both evolve, you can continue to assess whether you belong together for the long-term.

When you're in your twenties and the long-term thinking part of your brain is still evolving, you naturally look for 'Mr Right Now'. When you're older, you'll be better equipped to find 'Mr Right'.

Lack of life experience poses the #1 obstacle to a successful marriage. Family therapists say that most young couples lack well-developed identities and the skills to resolve problems. Emotionally they're not equipped to understand themselves, so they lack the ability to talk about conflicts non-destructively without either withdrawing or blowing up.

Couples who marry early thus burden their lives with serious extra hurdles. Men and women who divorce in their twenties report that they had intensely romanticised visions of marriage.

The 57 per cent divorce rate among the eighteen plus is unsurprising when you review the body of research on young marriages. No matter who you are or where you live, delaying marriage has distinct benefits, according to sociologist Paul Amato and his colleagues at Pennsylvania State University, an institution known for large-scale quantitative research. In their scholarly book *Alone Together: How Marriage in America is Changing,* they report their finding that meeting and marrying at an older age improves a couple's chances at a successful marriage. Older couples are more stable and have a better sense of closeness. Because singles in their thirties are more confident and emotionally mature, their unions have a higher rate of survival than young marriages. Says Dr Amato:

> We found that the delay in marriage was actually a good thing and it improved the average marital quality by a fair amount. Older marriages (thirties versus twenties) were more cohesive in the sense that they did things together more often as a couple, and couples who married at older ages were less likely to report thinking about divorce or that their marriage was in trouble.[2]

Slow down, agrees Johns Hopkins University sociologist Andrew Cherlin, author of the book *The Marriage-Go-Round: The State of Marriage and the Family in America Today*. He counsels that in order to avoid suffering from the massive relationship chaos in society today, you should wait to experience life more and get to know yourself well, becoming your own person before deciding to live with anyone else.

Right now, can you look in the mirror and honestly say to yourself, 'I'm happy and complete right now'? If you answer 'I'm not sure', then give yourself the chance to learn and grow. By staying single longer, you'll give yourself a chance to become the woman you want to be.

Delaying marriage is a sign of greater wisdom. Given medical advances, you may well live into your eighties and nineties. That means that marriage is a decision that you'll have to live with for over half a century.

So don't let an early marriage with the wrong guy prevent you from meeting your soulmate. Even if you're with the right guy, you won't know it if you're not ready. And he won't know either.

It's great that modern men today are taking on more work around the home, but what's even more interesting is that the longer a woman has worked outside the house before having children, the more housework and cooking and childcare the man does. If you take your career seriously, so will he.[3]

And you have time. I do not exaggerate when I say that the only thing at stake is your future.

But what about Down Syndrome?

In encouraging women to bear children young, people often cite the spectre of Down Syndrome among children of older moms. It's often said that a woman at the age of thirty-five has five times the chance of having a Down Syndrome baby than she did at the age of twenty. That sounds scary indeed. But statistics can be used to tell the story you want to tell. You could present the very same Down Syndrome numbers this way:

- At the age of twenty, a woman's chance of delivering a baby without Down Syndrome is 99.95 per cent.
- At the age of thirty-five, a woman's chance of delivering a baby without Down Syndrome is 99.75 per cent.
- At the age of forty-five, a woman's chance of delivering a baby without Down Syndrome is 97 per cent.[4]

As a woman ages, her overall risk of conceiving a child with Down Syndrome and similar genetic abnormalities remains very small, much smaller than the risks of other problems such as divorce and marital unhappiness if she marries too young.

In any case, if this is an issue that concerns you, you should know about the available prenatal tests to check for Down Syndrome and other genetic abnormalities in the early stages of pregnancy. That means if a woman chooses not to have a child with Down Syndrome, she never will have to, regardless of her age.

Looming infertility is often cited as another reason that women should bear children young. Much of the news on this issue can be traced back to a widely disseminated *New England Journal of Medicine* editorial recommending that women consider delaying their careers in order to have children earlier. That editorial is based on a 1982 French study supposedly demonstrating a 40 per cent increase in infertility in women in their early thirties.

After that French study was published, however, it was widely debunked in scientific circles, leading Princeton University's Office of Population Research to warn that the study could lead to 'needless anxiety' and 'costly medical treatment'.

In the journal *Family Planning Perspectives*, researcher John Bongaarts points out that the one-year time period used in the French study was misleading, since women often conceive after more than one year of trying. Additionally, he notes that the study's exclusive use of artificial insemination, done to control factors such as frequency of sex, was itself misleading, since women in natural sexual unions have a higher fertility rate than shown in the study.[5]

Even the original French researchers retreated from their own study, saying that their findings were not meant to apply to all women. However, neither their retreat nor all the disparagement of their fellow scientists has been widely reported in the media.[6]

Critics from throughout the medical establishment have since demanded a retraction of the *New England Journal of Medicine* editorial, shouting, 'How dare you write an editorial and upset people that way?'

Yale School of Medicine's Dr Alan DeCherney, who wrote the *New England Journal of Medicine* editorial, defended it, saying that even if the French study did have flaws, the study appeared 'better than some other ways' of doing fertility studies. In his words:

> Editorials are not always based on specific facts. They're written to make people think. I wouldn't change my

> life because of this study—there's very little data for one side or the other. But we wanted to be provocative and make people think and we hoped to make people look at the problem in greater depth.

What an extraordinarily flimsy and irresponsible way to frame an editorial opinion which has caused such fear and upset in women's lives!

I went looking for the facts, and I found that, even now, three decades later, most of the discussion takes the form of simple, unscientifically-based warnings to women similar to that of the *New England Journal of Medicine* editorial.

The largest and most recent research appears to be a 2005 study by the US National Center for Health Statistics, of 8,000 American women who were married and not using artificial insemination. It found that:

- For women age fifteen to twenty-nine, the infertility rate for the first child is 11 per cent and for later children, 4 per cent.
- For women age thirty to thirty-four, the infertility rate for the first child is 17 per cent and for later children, 6 per cent.
- For women age thirty-five to thirty-nine, the infertility rate for the first child is 23 per cent, and for later children, 4 per cent.
- For women age forty to forty-four, the infertility rate for the first child is 27 per cent, and for later children, 7 per cent.

This study is considered far more scientific than the 1982 French study, and the numbers are far less frightening. Even this study, though, uses the standard medical definition of infertility: A married couple is classified as 'infertile' if they have not used contraception and not become pregnant for twelve months or more.

In other words, even this study showing much lower rates of infertility does not control for either the fact that most couples have less sex in their thirties than in their twenties, or that many of these couples do become pregnant after twelve months. How much those two important factors impact the data and how early and how rapidly a woman's ability to bear children declines, nobody really knows.

Clearly, a woman's body becomes increasingly less fertile as she proceeds through her thirties and forties. Nobody really knows at what age this process starts to speed up and how quickly it takes place, but apparently it occurs significantly later than is commonly hyped.

For your own sake and for the sake of your future children, think before you rush into new relationships, think again before rushing into marriage and think again before bearing children. My point here is not that you should wait as long as possible, but that you should take a closer look before making major life decisions based on commonly accepted social dogma.

As for me, I had no trouble getting pregnant at ages thirty-nine and forty-one, and my babies were born healthy and beautiful. While I didn't plan my life this way, I am grateful that I did not marry and have kids too young. I'm a better woman—and wife and mother—for having given myself the chance to grow up first. The renowned child psychologist Dr Vicki Panaccione eloquently sums up my own feelings about the joys of being an older parent:[7]

Younger parents still have lots of life experiences to live, and can actually end up resenting the restrictions and responsibilities placed on them by virtue of having a child. Older parents tend to be more ready to settle down and focus their attention on the enjoyment of being parents and not feeling they are 'missing out' on other experiences. Their lives tend to be richer, and their experiences with each other, their children and life in general, have deeper meaning and appreciation.

Older parents tend to be more financially stable and secure in their careers, and have completed their education. This tends to mean less conflict regarding how to parcel out time, not having to juggle school, family and job. They also may be able to retire earlier, or be more flexible in their established work situation, affording them the opportunity to spend more time with their children.

Finally, older parents tend to be in more stable marriages, either because they have been together a long time, or have come together later in life with a clearer understanding of what they had been seeking in a life partner. They are more apt to have greater ability to communicate with each other, and have learned the importance of compromise and establishing agreement. In child rearing, this is particularly important. Stable relationships provide greater stability for children. And, relationships developing later in life tend to be more passionate, and passionate partners make better parents.

Your daddy wants to get you adopted by a sugar daddy

I hear from a lot of readers whose parents want to decide whom they marry. This is from a male reader:

> Joy, my girlfriend and I were together for almost one year. My parents didn't approve because her family background is not great. So I broke up with her. To be honest, I really loved her. When we broke up, I cried and she cried. After a time, my uncle called and told me about a friend who is very rich and owns many factories. The friend has a daughter who is an only child. My parents tell me that feelings of love take time to develop and the other family's background is excellent. They want me to be a good son and marry this girl. What should I do?

And this from a female reader:

> For a long time, my friend wanted to marry the man she really loved. But her parents never approved of it and would not let her. So she married someone else for a short time and got divorced, the logic being that after the divorce she would be worthless and her parents would reluctantly have to accept her choice in marriage. The resulting scandal was so huge that the grief almost killed her mother.

These are extremely difficult situations. For thousands of years until now in our society, marriage spoke to the needs of larger groups. A woman's marriage decision was based not on love or partnership but instead on family considerations. By strategically marrying off their sons and daughters, wealthy families consolidated their wealth, merged resources and forged political alliances. Marriage was for lineage and security and women lived to please others.

Your parents may or may not be looking at your marriage as a strategic family matter. Still, if they're like most parents, they worry about you. You're their precious daughter. And that's why they want to get you married off, ASAP, preferably to a rich man. Ideally, your future husband is a combination of a multi-millionaire, gourmet chef, family doctor and multiple-passport holder. Your parents want to someday rest in peace knowing you are safe and secure. Daddy wants to get you safely adopted by a sugar daddy.

The struggle over who makes the decision of whether, when and whom you marry is at the absolute crux of all the deep historical and cultural storms swirling around us as women today. At the heart of that struggle are you and your parents.

After thinking long and hard about this issue, I can't come to any other conclusion than this: Being a modern woman today means that you must make your own marriage decision.

I don't make this statement lightly. This is the biggest decision of your entire life, and the people who will be most impacted by this decision are not your parents, but you and your future husband and any future children you might have together.

The marriage decision is a milestone in the overall evolution of your relationship with your parents. In fact, as you mature, the major relationship in your life that will change is the one you have with your parents.

An important part of growing up is learning to see your parents in a new light. Learn to see your parents as people and not just as your parents. They are not the omniscient, all-powerful people you once thought they were.

Parents are just people who happened to have children. They're human, with human abilities and human failings. They have problems of their own, which may not be too different from the problems that you face. They may not have been perfect parents, but they probably did the best they could.

In your mind, they need to shift from being the primary authority over your life to being one piece of a broader support system which now includes your friends, colleagues and everyone around you. You're all adults now. This new relationship can allow you and them to establish even closer bonds of intimacy and friendship.

Don't just rebel. Simply being contrary is worse than letting their expectations rule your life. They'll always have more experience than you and can offer valuable perspectives, so let them love and support you and give you their opinions.

But know that whether or not you're financially independent, you now are 100 per cent responsible for your own life. That also means you need to stop blaming them for what's wrong in your life and for the pressure in your life. They've done their job, and now you're officially an adult. Now you're in charge.

Independence means independence from your parents

After all, what does it mean to be 'independent'? Implicit in the term are your parents, since they're the 'from whom' you're releasing your dependence. It's up to you to transform yourself so that you're not simply a reflection of them.

In the same way, they need to learn to see you as an individual and not simply as their child. Go easy on them. As hard a transition as this is for you, it may be even harder for them. After all, they've spent over two decades taking care of you, and while your drive for independence feels natural to you, to them it may seem sudden.

The moment I became a mother, at the first sight of my precious baby, I experienced pure joy and love, just like in the movies. But my tears also included an emotion I didn't expect: Fear. I thought, my God, how in the world am I going to protect this tiny life and keep her safe? I realised then that I had no idea how to be a mother.

Recently, a sickening traffic accident took place in my neighbourhood. A mother walked out of her house, leaving the door ajar. She got into her car, put it into reverse—and crushed her two-year-old daughter who had quietly followed her out the door.

It was a brief news item in the local newspaper. The article didn't include a photo. But when I read the piece my mind instantly recreated it as a horror movie played in agonising slow motion. In the weeks since, that movie has continued to infiltrate my consciousness because it strikes at the most elemental terror in the heart of every parent in the world.

As a parent, you just want to know that your kid is going to be OK. You think about her all the time. You'd do anything to make her life easier and happier.

I share with you this vignette because as you develop your relationship with your parents, it's important that you learn to empathise with them. Being a parent means living with your heart outside of your body.

It's a long way off for me as a mother, but already I think, with a mixture of hope and dread, of the day when it will be time to let go of my daughters and watch them venture out into the world.

At that time, I'll just have to trust them to make the right decisions—though I hope they will consult with me a lot. Someday, I know I'll learn first-hand that the very hardest part of parenting is letting go.

Reflecting on his cancer and life, Steve Jobs said:

> Your time is limited, so don't waste it living someone else's life. Don't be trapped by dogma, which is living with the results of other people's thinking. Don't let the noise of other's opinions drown out your own inner voice. And most important, have the courage to follow your heart and intuition. They somehow already know what you truly want to become. Everything else is secondary.

For us as women, the process of growing up is the process of separating ourselves mentally, emotionally and spiritually from the pressures around us. Now is the time to start setting your own standards and living by them.

Chapter 15

Love the World

Don't just curse the darkness. Light a fire.

—Chai Jing

Recently on the radio, I heard a story about an unusual hobby. The hobbyists, all men, take used cars, seal up the windows, remove the seats, then stuff the cars full with stereo equipment so powerful that if you listen to the music, you will go deaf.

In their competitions, each man sits in his car with headphones on to protect his ears, drives his car three metres to show it works, then stops the car and turns up the music as loud as it can go. A testing machine in his car measures the decibel level inside. The man whose car plays the loudest music, wins.

The radio reporter attended one of these competitions and interviewed the winner, asking on behalf of us all, 'Heck, you can't even use this car to take a girl out on a date to impress her! You spend all this time and money on a car that plays music so loud that nobody can listen to it! So why?'

The man replied, 'Because now I can say I'm #1 at something.'

So touching! And yet, I thought when I heard this story, so meaningless!

The truth is, it's easy to get caught up in meaningless competition, for money or success or fame. I know I certainly have.

Readers sometimes ask me, 'What is the meaning of life?'

This is obviously a really personal and subjective matter.

I believe that as humans we're hard-wired for love. I believe that each of us is part of a larger whole and that to be truly happy and to achieve meaning we have to join ourselves to that larger whole. We do this by making the world a better place. Only when we work with others and help others do we feel spiritually healthy and human. To feel good we have to do good.

Does that sound idealistic?

After all, if everyone else is behaving selfishly, and yet we behave selflessly, are we just being chumps? That's essentially what one reader once asked me:

> In India and China, drastic socio-economic transition has brought about society-wide loss of direction. Many good values are lost. Money and consumption reign. Our parents sacrificed for us to be successful. Should we, therefore, focus on being successful or on changing the world?

Good question, and one I've struggled with myself.

The tragedy of the commons in American politics

Once I became an official at Los Angeles City Hall, I was stunned at the magnitude of the power and money flowing through its marbled corridors. It took over US $10 billion each year to operate the city and our related airports and harbours. We were embarking on an expansion of LAX airport worth another US $11 billion. Our decades-old water and power infrastructure was in constant need of repair. Our municipal rail system was always in need of new tunnels and railcars. There were grand, architecturally trendsetting municipal buildings needed to house the Mayor and 50,000 city employees. And let's not forget the tens of billions of dollars of pension fund monies that needed to be invested and municipal bond obligations that needed to be issued.

Then and now, all this spending attracts construction firms, investment banks and all sorts of other companies from all over the world lusting for city contracts and willing to send a little back to any city official who send contract dollars their way.

Such trades need not be handled as inelegantly as with envelopes of cash, which could get everyone sent to jail. The disbursements come back in the form of campaign donations, or as jobs and internships for officials' children or spouses, or as jobs or consulting assignments for the officials themselves after they leave office.

Many officials leave office for lucrative jobs as lobbyists helping companies gain insider access to those city contracts. In American politics, we even have a term for the practice of rotating between insider governmental positions and influence-peddling lobbyist jobs, 'The revolving door'.

The fact is, when you're a top official in a big city in US, the personal economic opportunities are everywhere.

All this makes working as a high-level official in city government a great place to consider the meaning of life. To work amidst so much power and money is to be constantly confronted with ethical gray areas. Through the large and small decisions that you make each day, you define who you are and what kind of world you want to live in.

The situation sets up what economists refer to as 'the tragedy of the commons'. If you have a town full of farmers and a town commons full of grass, it's in each farmer's interest to put his cows on the commons rather than on his own land, even though, over time, the commons becomes degraded through overgrazing. That's because each farmer receives all the benefits from grazing his own cows on the commons, while the damage to the commons is shared by everyone.

It's an apt analogy for the corrosive influence of money in politics in America. Every day, the people work hard to be productive and to pay taxes to a government whose job is to serve them. And yet, over time, public officials turn their backs on the people and instead serve themselves and the companies who line their pockets. The corruption is systemic.

The whole situation is enough to make any rational person feel angry, helpless and hopeless. I did sometimes ask myself, can one person make a difference? And if not, what's the point of even trying?

I won't lie to you. Watching other farmers graze their cows on the town commons did sometimes make me wonder, when others are getting away with corruption, why should I be good?

Why shouldn't I take advantage of the opportunity to quietly set myself up? If I don't graze my cows on the town commons, am I just being a chump? Besides, I had to take a pay cut from the business world to come work in public service. Why should I suffer financially for serving the people? Shouldn't I provide for my parents and any future husband and children I might have? (PR tip: It's always nicer to frame any misdeeds in the context of taking care of one's family.)

Such were the thoughts rolling around my head as I entered office and looked ahead to the challenges looming ahead of me as a public servant.

As deputy mayor, I was responsible for economic and workforce development, so when I got started I ordered our city's first ever study of adult education levels of our people. What we found shocked even the experts who conducted the study. 53 per cent of our working-age adults lacked the literacy to read street signs or bus schedules, or to complete a job application in English. This was higher than in any other big city in the US, and I'm guessing it's higher than in any big city in China or India.

While Los Angeles is known as the world's glamour capital, the reality is that if you graph the city's residents by wealth, you'll see a lopsided barbell of rich and poor. The 'beautiful people' here in fact are far outnumbered by Central American and South Asian immigrants who come to escape lives of poverty and deprivation. They work as our gardeners, dishwashers and construction labourers.

In this respect, Los Angeles is different from New York. Most immigrants come to New York on airplanes, but they come to Los Angeles on foot. Ours are poorer and more desperate. Many lack literacy in any language—English or their language of origin.

Low literacy has cascading effects on people and their families. Not surprisingly, people with low literacy are low-income, since good jobs require literacy. They have a hard time getting around town. They have poor physical health.

All this presents them with a huge number of daily logistical challenges, but what I found equally poignant was how their poor reading skills stunt their spiritual and emotional lives.

Their experience made me recall my own childhood in the US when I also felt I had no native language. I learned the English of my textbooks, but that was a language full of facts and figures. We spoke Chinese around the house, so I knew the words for foods and other household items. But since we rarely discussed feelings, I never learned how to express myself in Chinese either. I was a no-no girl. Neither my Chinese nor my English was adequate for expressing all the feelings I had bottled up inside. I can't tell you how sad and frustrating this was for me. Each year, my soul grew wilder and more pained, lacking a way to converse with the world or, indeed, even with myself.

So I became a reader, learning through other people's stories. I consumed books voraciously, in English, peering into the rich emotional lives of great writers and the characters they imagined. It was through their words that

I acquired the words to express myself. From there, I went on to Duke, where I was richly educated in the humanities and social sciences. I devoured all kinds of subjects ranging from anthropology to comparative religion to literature from all ages and cultures. Following Duke, I went on to UCLA, where I gained broad learning across the worlds of business and of urban planning.

My education taught me to think. Without learning how to think, I would not have achieved anything else that I've achieved since then. And I could not have learned to think without first acquiring the words to do so.

So it was then, when I was suddenly confronted with the magnitude of our city's education problem, I was especially affected by the assault on the basic humanity of each of my neighbours plagued by low literacy. I couldn't imagine what it would be like not to be able to read a single great book. I couldn't imagine walking past a news stand and feeling intimidated by the explosion of printed words. I couldn't imagine feeling ashamed when my kids surpassed me in reading ability. I couldn't imagine not being able to help my kids with their schoolwork.

That's why I found my work in education so deeply motivating and fun. Helping people attain literacy meant not only helping them towards financial and physical security, but also giving them the key to unlock their own humanity. The programmes I created to expand literacy and college access became models that have since been replicated across California.

In fact, every time I've given myself to the world, I've received more than I've given.

Be successful or change the world?

So here's my answer to the blog reader who asked me whether we should be successful or change the world. This is a false dichotomy. You become successful by changing the world.

To make the world a better place you don't have to become poor. And you don't have to wait until you first get rich and powerful.

As human beings, we're programmed to pursue meaning. Meaning does not come from money. Says London Business School professor Gary Hamel, 'As an emotional catalyst, wealth maximisation lacks the power to fully mobilise human energies.'[1]

Meaning comes from doing work that matters. We need, as Steve Jobs urges, to 'make a ding in the universe'. Truly successful people allocate their resources in service of something bigger than themselves.

The world is stuffed full with so many problems that it's easy to despair over the enormity of them all. It's easy even to worsen the problems, rationalising that at least you can take care of yourself and your loved ones while the rest of the world goes to seed. It's easy to get caught up in wanting what we don't have that we forget all that we do have. Such as when I was growing up in the US, the world's richest country, attending the world's best schools, and all I wanted was to be white. Such as when I was in my twenties in Los Angeles, free and healthy and with a life full of adventure and friends, and all I wanted was—more. More power, more money, more prestige, more of anything that I didn't already have.

The truth is, the world is a completely unfair place. There are billions—literally billions—of people in this world who would love to have been given what I've been given. People in poor countries, and people right here in the US who lack basic skills. Nothing about me made me more deserving than any one of them.

The only way I know to acknowledge and honour this fact is to do work that matters.

We're all in this world together. The way to be truly happy and to achieve meaning is to instigate the change that we wish for in the world.

They say that Americans always want to change the world while Asians are only out for themselves. But I look around and see staggering evidence to the contrary. I am constantly moved by the beautiful voices of the writers and artists and others out there envisioning a better India and China. I see the disaster-relief, child-location and other volunteer efforts popping up everywhere around India and China. I see how people naturally strain towards finding ways to leave their communities a little better than before.

And changing the world is incredibly fun. As the Singaporean-Chinese-American Google engineer Chade-Meng ('Meng') Tan said in his wonderful TED talk at the United Nations, 'Compassion is not a chore. Compassion is something that creates happiness. Compassion is fun!'[2]

In his talk, Meng tells us about the world's happiest man, Matthieu Ricard, a Buddhist monk and the son of a renowned French philosopher. When neurologists measure happiness through brain activity, Matthieu Ricard scores by far as the happiest man in the world.

Which leads one to wonder, What was he thinking about when he was being measured? Something naughty, perhaps? No, actually, he was thinking about compassion. It turns out that compassion is the happiest thing ever.

What's more, compassion creates highly effective business leaders. Compassion reduces our natural tendencies towards self-obsession because, in Meng's words, 'The cognitive and affective components of compassion are understanding people and empathising with people.' Compassion builds our capacity for the #1 leadership skill, empathy.

When you approach life from a standpoint of abundance and of connection to others, you will have more success in all that you do. When you share yourself with the world, you will always get back more.

To find your voice, create something. To infuse your life with meaning and fun and to grow your leadership skills, do good for others. So consolidate your efforts and create something of value to the world.

For inspiration, we can look to the example of Yue-Sai Kan. Yue-Sai is famous for being stunningly beautiful, but what I find most stunning about her is her deep inner humanity. For three decades, she's created amazing new things—TV programming, cosmetics, books—which lift hearts and teach us how to be modern.

By now, she's achieved so much that no one would fault her for relaxing and enjoying the fruits of her hard work. But she's not done. She continues to work tirelessly, leveraging all of her fame and power, to infuse the world with more of what the world needs right now: Beauty, honour, grace, style and love. The world is a better place thanks to her.

It's so yesterday to let the world define you by your marital status. Establish yourself as a woman to watch. Create something of value. Shock them with how amazing, how special, how luminous is your contribution. Because it's a reflection of you.

Your remarkable works will create magic. When you unleash your creativity and create something honest and true—something that comes from deep inside of you, that helps other people and that you share effectively—amazing things will happen.

New friends will show up in your life, people who see in your work a glimpse of themselves. Fellow creative travellers who love the same things you do.

And they will bring you unexpected new opportunities for collaboration. Opportunities that are perfectly suited to them and perfectly suited to you and which you never could have imagined on your own. Then you will partner with them to create value that no one person could create alone. It happened to me. My blog brought to me every person listed in this book's Acknowledgements who is not a member of my family.

Over time, as you break out of the boxes that society put you in, you'll achieve more than you previously had imagined in all aspects of your life. You'll accomplish what you set out to do. You'll be a part of leading innovation in your country.

Then, someday, a journalist will stick a microphone in your face and ask, 'They said Asians couldn't innovate their way out of a paper bag! How did you create something so special?

And you'll reply simply, 'I followed my heart.'

Being good has nothing to do with how many men you've had sex with

Now, you're probably wondering, 'What? We were just talking about the meaning of life. How did we suddenly switch subjects to how many men you've had sex with? Did Joy have a memory lapse? Did the publisher mis-number the pages of this book?'

No. There is no mistake. And yes, it makes no sense to evaluate a woman based on the number of men she's had sex with.

Recently, I was chatting with a friend in Beijing, who had just come from a party where a guy said this:

> If a woman has had sex with three or more men and I marry her, she can't blame me if later I have sex with other women.

This quote has stuck in my mind. It describes a world in which women are nothing more than sex objects for men.

A world in which men establish all the rules and women have no choice but to submit to those rules. A world in which the abuse and debasement of women is commonplace. A world in which human beings relate to one another by using one another. A cold and brutal world lacking humanity and devoid of love.

So here we are, living in this strange yet exciting moment in history. When chauvinism still rules in some corners, but when in our hearts we know that, as women, every one of us has just as much right to dignity as any other human being.

Let us be clear. Sex has nothing to do with morality. Morality has nothing to do with sex. Morality has to do with whether we are kind and fair and compassionate with the people around us.

When we treat other people well, we are behaving morally. When we abuse other people, we are behaving immorally. By this measure, the above quote is immoral.

As women, we must learn to see ourselves as more than sex objects or pre-wives or pre-mothers or daughters or wives or mothers. The only way to defeat the chauvinism surrounding us is for each of us to start ignoring the rules, and instead to start truly connecting, with our own selves, and with those around us.

It's our turn now

Ladies, don't falter now. We're at the vanguard. We've studied too much, worked too hard, sacrificed too much, to get to where we are right now, at this particular point in history and in our lives. We have nothing to lose and everything to gain.

By linking arms, we can go where no one else has gone and do what no one else has done: Move our society away from hierarchy to the edge of possibility.

We can be the planners and architects of a glittering new society, bound by our rules this time. Where women and men all are free as butterflies. Where women are free to achieve and men are free to love. Where love does not result in the punishment and death of the lovers. Where we all can discover our own humanity. Where children are born free.

Asia will be a better place as a result of our leadership.

The act of creating anything new is by its nature creative, improvisational, starting from the familiar and heading off into the unknown. It's the same with all art and science. We have no models but the ones which we ourselves create. We'll use our imaginations.

Acknowledgements

Two years ago when I had just started the Global Rencai blog, my editor Tangtang Man envisioned a book for women even before I envisioned myself a professional writer. Tangtang seduced me into taking on this creative endeavour and then prodded it into reality.

Along the way, Linyan Zhou was my researcher and thought partner as I laboured to wrestle vague ideas into coherent thoughts and then to put them into logical order. Linyan's beautiful mind is matched by her beautiful soul. This book benefited from both.

As the manuscript took shape, Yingying Zhang, Lingyi Sun, Yanting Wang, Zhang Ying, Erin Qin, Jun Deng, Haodong Chen, Tina Wang and Jingjing Song served as reviewers, providing me with valuable input. Each of these young talents is headed for big things, so watch out world.

Just as I am not a professional writer, Ivy Wang is not a professional translator, We're just a couple of women with a shared passion for the written word. Ivy made my heart sing as together we revelled in the intricacies of the Chinese and English languages. The lyricism of the language in this book is testament to Ivy's prodigious talent, as well as to her infinite patience with my countless edits.

More than anyone else, my husband Dave made this book possible. As I set aside my headhunting business to write, Dave alone has supported our family through his business. What's more, a thousand times when I disappeared exclaiming, 'Not now, Mama's busy writing!' he did double dad duty. Dave always has urged me to chase my dreams even while encouraging our little girls to start forming dreams of their own. If this is a book about dreams and about true love, my Dave for me is the personification of both.

Finally, I thank all of my loyal blog readers who from the start have lifted me up with their constant support and inspiration. Dear readers, this is your book too.

Dave Has Something to Say

Joy and I first met at a little beach restaurant in Los Angeles. Right away I was attracted to Joy's special charm, a beauty powered by her warm and playful spirit. That evening, we talked for hours. I had the feeling that my life was about to be changed forever by this little Chinese woman with the big heart.

A year later when Joy and I married, she made me the world's happiest man.

Joy is the perfect woman for me, but she might not fit some men's vision of an ideal wife. Specifically:

- **Joy knows nothing about professional sports.** I'm a sports lover but Joy is not. When we first met, I tried to incite her competitive instincts by saying that her sports knowledge was within the bottom 2 per cent of all Americans. She never took the bait. Nowadays, she continues to confuse the San Francisco Giants, the baseball team, with the New York Giants, my football team. She has a hard time keeping track of how points are scored in any team sport. I've given up trying to change her in this respect.

- **Joy does not cook.** At all. When I read that in her twenties, Joy ate a lot of ramen, I had to laugh. That's because ramen is cheap, but also because to cook ramen, you need to know only how to boil water. By now, four years and two kids into our marriage, she's made some progress. She makes scrambled eggs. And she makes ice cream, by mixing milk, sugar and eggs into the deluxe ice cream making machine that our friends bought us. Does ice cream making count as cooking?
- **Joy is not handy around the house.** Once when we were dating, she asked me to fix something that had broken in her beautiful downtown apartment. I asked if she had a toolbox. Surprisingly, she did. Unsurprisingly, it looked like a museum showpiece, 15 cm x 60 cm x 10 cm tall, a deep, velvety red, smooth and shiny, without a dent or smudge or any sign of use. Inside it contained one single solitary hammer. No screwdrivers, no wrenches, no tape measures, no nails. I wondered, what does one do with a hammer and no nails? Her response was, 'The picture-hanging kits come with the nails but not the hammer.'

So you can see why some may regard Joy as an impractical choice as a wife. She is obviously and enormously talented, but she's lopsided. She focuses on some things and completely ignores other things. She's her own unique self. A woman brimming with passion and ideas. A dreamer.

When Joy started writing her blog, I saw it as a great creative outlet and a smart way for her to connect with many interesting young talents. Good for her business, and good for the world.

But then Tangtang asked her to write a book, and I started to worry.

Then Joy wanted to take leave from her business to write this book, and I started to worry more.

What about money?

What about our family?

What about me?

To further complicate things, at the time, America was entering a massive recession, and my industry, real estate development, was suffering. I'd just completed renovating two apartment buildings, prices were starting to slide, and I was scrambling to negotiate the final sales before the recession gobbled up the buildings.

All that put a lot of pressure on us, and especially on me. But it became obvious that this book project was deeply important to Joy. I realised that when you fall in love, the adjustments you make are not that hard because in your heart you want to support every ambition that person has. With Joy that's exactly how I feel.

And so a year ago, I agreed to double my efforts and support our family while she put her business on hold.

Early on, it became obvious that Joy could not write at home with the babies constantly tugging at her leg, and so we rented her a one-room office nearby. That sometimes meant my coming home early from work to be with our girls. Looking back on this year, I'm glad to have had that extra time to bond with them in a way that many fathers never get to.

Joy did not limit her writing to normal business hours. She worked around the clock. Many nights, I awoke in the middle of the night to see her face lit up by the glow of her smartphone as she tapped out book notes with her thumbs. I tried to ban smartphones from our bedroom, but by now you know that Joy doesn't easily follow the arbitrary rules of others.

There were times in the past year when I did wonder. I wondered if this was just nothing more than a personal creative project. I wondered if anyone would ever read this book, and if it would make a difference to any person other than Joy. I wondered if we would look back on this year as a year wasted or a year gained.

At the same time, I saw how Joy connected with her readers. I saw how their eyes lit up when they met her in person. I saw the joy that she spread in their lives and in the lives of their friends. I saw that Joy has a special gift, and a special opportunity to touch lives through the power of her words.

Joy is not a typical wife. In her lifetime, she's had unusual experiences. Yet in the overall arc of her life, she's faced many of the same struggles that face all women today. It takes courage to write so personally about those struggles. I'm proud of Joy for her creation.

Joy is an incredible life partner in so many ways that I could not list them all here. It seems we're always together talking and laughing, whether we're walking along the streets of New York or cleaning up crayons scattered around the house. Each new day is packed with adventure.

Our girls are growing up with the example of a mother who balances it all with compelling grace. The world may see Joy as a thinker and leader, but at home we see the private side of her. Joy packs our house full of love and laughter. We're always receiving family and friends who share in and contribute to the joy of our home. Our lives are surrounded with the love and friendship of amazing women and men doing great things in the world. Nurtured in this environment, our little girls are starting to blossom into their own independent and charming selves.

Guys—and I know you're out there because this book is the best inside peek into the mysteries of women—I'll give you one piece of advice. Have your fun dating around, but when it's time for a life partner, mature women are better.

Dave

Postscript from Joy:

Ladies, you have no need for a toolbox at all. Need something fixed? Be practical. Call a guy friend, your boyfriend or your husband. Men are so charming. They love to help!

I have not yet found all of life's answers but I have found one important answer in Dave. I'm grateful that to have a whole second lifetime ahead with him by my side.

I wish for you every good thing. May you go out and find the joy in who you are and in all that this world has to offer.

Endnotes

Introduction

1. iFeng.com report on a study by Tsinghua University and *Inside China* on marriage and divorce in China, http://fashion.ifeng.com/emotion/topic/detail_2013_02/19/22252432_0.shtml
2. Zhou, Yun and Ren, Qiang, 'Longevity Among Chinese Consanguines,' in *Longer Life and Healthy Aging*. Zeng, Yi, ed. 2006.
3. Birrin, James, 'The Process of Aging,' in *Our Aging Society: Paradox and Promise*. Pifer, Alan and Bronte, Lydia, eds. 1986.
4. Heilbrun, Carolyn G, *Writing a Woman's Life*, 1989.

Chapter 1

1. Damst, Alison, 'For Chinese Women, US MBAs are All the Rage,' *Bloomberg Businessweek*, May 2011.

Chapter 2

1. Akst, Daniel, 'Roommate Not Wanted,' *The Wall Street Journal*, 29 January 2012.
2. Roberts, Sam, '51 per cent of Women are Now Living Without Spouse,' *New York Times*, 16 January 2007.
3. iFeng, ibid.

Chapter 3

1. Marano, Hara Estroff, 'Marriage Math', *Psychology Today*, 16 March 2004, reviewed on 23 July 2010.

Chapter 4

1. Offer, Shira and Schneider, Barbara, 'Revisiting the Gender Gap in Time-use Patterns: Multitasking and Well-being among Mothers and Fathers in Dual-earner Families', *American Sociological Review*, December 2011, http://www.asanet.org/images/journals/docs/pdf/asr/Dec11ASRFeature.pdf
2. http://www.shwanda.net/knowledge/13.html
3. What is Your Mom Worth?' *Salary.com*, 2011, http://swz.salary.com/momsalarywizard/htmls/mswl_momcenter.html
4. Steinem, Gloria. *Doing Sixty and Seventy*. 2006.

Chapter 5

1. Csikszentmihalyi, Mihaly, 'The Creative Personality,' *Psychology Today*, 1 July 1996, reviewed on 13 June 2011.
2. Debold, Elizabeth, 'Flow with Soul: An interview with Dr Mihaly Csikszentmihalyi', *Enlightenment Next*, Spring-Summer 2002, http://www.enlightennext.org/magazine/j21/csiksz.asp

Chapter 6

1. Bower, Joseph L and Gilbert, Clark G. *From Resource Allocation to Strategy*. 2006.

Chapter 7

1. Ben-Shahar, Tal. *Happier: Learn the Secrets to Daily Joy and Lasting Fulfillment*. 2007.

Chapter 8

1. Rudin, Mike, 'The Science of Happiness', *BBC*, 30 April 2006, http://news.bbc.co.uk/2/hi/programmes/happiness_formula/4783836.stm
2. 'With Age Comes Happiness, University of Chicago Study Shows', University of Chicago press release, 16 April 2008, http://news.uchicago.edu/article/2008/04/16/age-comes-happiness-university-chicago-study-shows

Chapter 9

1. Branigan, Tania, 'Manager Becomes First Man Jailed Under Chinese Harassment Laws', *The Guardian*, 16 July 2008.
2. http://blog.penelopetrunk.com/2006/11/02/dont-report-sexual-harassment-in-most-cases/

Chapter 11

1. 'Plain Dealer Columnist Regina Brett Shares 50 Lessons Learned in Her New Book on Navigating Life's Detours,' *The Plain Dealer*, 10 April 2010, http://www.cleveland.com/brett/blog/index.ssf/2010/04/plain_dealer_columnist_regina.html

Chapter 14

1. Henig, Robin Marantz, 'What is it about 20-somethings?' *The New York Times*, 18 August 2010.
2. Gershuny, Jonathan I; Bittman, Michael and Brice, John, 'Exit, Voice and Suffering: Do Couples Adapt to Changing Employment Patterns?' *Journal of Marriage and Family*, 2005.
3. 'Too Young to Get Married? See What the Experts Say,' National Healthy Marriage Resource Center, a project funded by the US Department of Health and Human Services, Administration for Children and Families, http://www.twoofus.org/educational-content/articles/too-young-to-get-married-see-what-the-experts-say/index.aspx
4. Sears, William, MD and Sears, Martha, RN, 'How Frequently Does Down Syndrome Occur?' *AskDrSears.com*, http://www.askdrsears.com/topics/child-rearing-and-development/down-syndrome/how-frequently-does-down-syndrome-occur
5. Webster, Bayard, 'Methods Disputed in Fertility Study', *The New York Times*, 21 March 1982, http://www.nytimes.com/1982/03/21/us/methods-disputed-in-fertility-study.html
6. Faludi, Susan. *Backlash: The Undeclared War Against American Women*. 1992.
7. Panaccione, Vicki, 'The Advantages of Being an Older Parent', 12 January 2011, http://www.betterparentinginstitute.com/Better-Parenting/parenting-child-raising-skills/advantages-of-being-older-parents/

Chapter 15

1. Hamel, Gary, 'Moon Shots for Management', *Harvard Business Review*, February 2009.
2. Tan, Chade-Meng, 'Everyday Compassion at Google', *TED Talk*, 2011, http://www.ted.com/talks/chade_meng_tan_everyday_compassion_at_google.html